WE BELIEVE

A Small-Town's Journey to the Little League World Series

E V A N   S A T I N O F F

We Believe

©2023, Evan Satinoff

ISBN: 979-8-35091-248-7

ISBN eBook: 979-8-35091-249-4

CONTENTS

FOREWORD

To say the boys on the '22 team looked up to the kids on the '21 team would be an understatement. Now, they played it cool like they didn't, but they did, especially early in the summer. All the '22 boys watched every second of every game that ESPN aired on its network. They knew the games from the previous summer inside and out. They could recite every big pitch, big hit, and big play. Some of the boys knew Jack and William, but many didn't, so they, too, were like mythical creatures to most of the '22 boys.

The '21 team's motto or battle cry was "One Team, One Dream!" Anyone who followed the team at all knew that, so when the '22 team was formed in early June 2022, that same motto carried over with the boys breaking every huddle, yelling that before they would sprint to their positions on the field or break it down for the evening. The boys loved it, and it created a bit of a connection between the two teams.

But things changed on Sunday, July 17. Evan will go into more detail later in the book, but the short story is we got beat 3-1 by Columbia early in the state tournament. Looking back at things, that was the turning point for this team. We shouldn't have lost the game. We left runners on in each inning, 10 total runners, in fact, in that six-inning game; plus, we had two guys thrown out on bang-bang plays at home. So, while it was super disappointing, the post-game chat wasn't filled with would haves, should haves, and could haves.

When the team gathered right after the game, the boys were deflated. They knew they had not capitalized on a number of opportunities during that game. But instead of just consoling the boys, we challenged them and asked them to believe. That moment is one we will remember forever. It's where the '22 team's battle cry came to be.

We knew it was going to be a long road to hoe. We would have to play and win five straight games over the next five days to win the state championship. That's a tall order even for the best of teams, but in that moment right after the game, two words changed the trajectory of the team: "We Believe!"

Randy believed. Evan believed. Mark believed. Now whether the boys did in that moment, who knows. But what happened that night and the days that followed built the momentum that we would ride for five consecutive games there in Goodlettsville. We went on to run-rule Columbia in the last two games that week to win the state tourney, and the rest, as they say, is history.

The boys and all our families believed as the boys, time and time again, came up clutch in the most crucial moments. Evan's recounting of the stories that are the 2022 Nolensville Little League All-Star team in the pages that follow is a treasure to all of us who lived it. We thank you for living it alongside us, and we hope you enjoy recounting the stories with us.

– Randy Huth and Mark Carter

PREFACE

Baseball, America's pastime, has been an integral part of my DNA as early as I can remember. Looking back, one of my all-time favorite pictures is of me as an infant, smiling ear to ear, wearing a red ball cap with a baseball set in front of my hands. That same vibrant smile appears 48 years later when I'm around the greatest sport on earth. For me, my love for baseball began as a young kid growing up in Palm Harbor, Florida. My dad, Elliot, a stickball legend from the Bronx, only knew one sport. I remember the early days when other sports were mentioned in conversation by family, friends, and even strangers, my dad would tenaciously proclaim there is no sport other than baseball. To this day, still, that strong sentiment remains intact.

My love for baseball began early

I started my baseball career as a Little Leaguer myself playing for Dunedin National Little League, soon moving over to Palm Harbor Recreation League. Typically coached by my all-time favorite, my dad, I spent countless hours at the ballpark with him and my mom and my brother. Throughout my childhood, baseball played such an important role in my life whether it was playing the sport, watching it, collecting baseball cards, or in many cases, just having passionate conversations about baseball in general.

Some of my favorite memories are of my brother and me hanging out at Englebert Complex in Dunedin, home of the Toronto Blue Jay's spring training site. We would visit the complex on Saturday mornings before the actual spring training games started just to watch the big leaguers practice their craft. On many occasions, we would head to the dumpster on the side of the complex, dive in, and, jubilantly, grab broken wooden bats thrown out by the clubhouse attendants.

This love of baseball didn't come by accident. It was passed down by both of my parents to my brother and me by unmatched means. Our childhood summer vacations didn't always consist of magical theme parks or paradise beach retreats. Rather, almost every summer, we would explore different baseball parks around the country. Many summers we would take an eight-hour trek up I-75 and travel to Atlanta to see the Braves take on some of the national league powerhouses. Most family road trips today consist of kids being self-occupied listening to their favorite music or playing non-stop games on their favorite Apple devices, but thirty-five years ago that so-called luxury was nonexistent, so what passed time was a competitive game of baseball trivia. The judge and baseball historian, my dad, would provide topics leading to an array of baseball-themed questions. To make it even more fun and competitive was the fact that money was always on the line. As if seeing a major league baseball game in person wasn't enough, my parents treated the Satinoff boys by staying at the Marriott Marquees located in downtown Atlanta, and it wasn't for its illustrious pool or scrumptious breakfast buffet. Instead, my parents made it a point to stay at this particular hotel for us to meet, mingle, and get autographs from opposing players since they knew that would be an absolute thrill for both Dan and me.

However, baseball wasn't just for summers. Living in Florida, playing some kind of baseball was a bit of a year-round routine. Around 6:00 p.m., before dinner and after a hard day's work, my dad would take my brother and me out to the street in front of our home. One of the all-time greatest fielding games, "Errors," originated in front of our home in Palm Harbor. My brother and I would line up approximately fifteen to twenty feet apart from my dad. With his infamous first baseman's glove in hand, Dad would throw a hard grounder to each of us on the asphalt street. He would move us to our forehand, then backhand, slow rollers, and pop ups. If one of us missed the ball, an "error" was shouted out. The first kid to get five errors was eliminated and the other brother was granted the winner of the game that evening. I carried over this childhood tradition with my kids, Ella, Jack, and William, to the streets and driveways of Florida, Ohio, North Carolina, Arizona, and now, Tennessee.

Throughout my childhood collecting baseball cards was not just a fun hobby for my brother and me, but rather a business for my family from 1986-1988. Cooperstown South, located off US 19 in Palm Harbor, Florida, was a shop where collectors of all ages could browse, buy, and trade baseball cards and memorabilia. After high school was let out, my brother operated the shop during the week, and periodically, I would do odd type jobs around the store on the weekends. Other than the diamond, this baseball shrine was a home away from home for my family and me.

Speaking of homes, when we initially moved to Palm Harbor in 1981, our home was like any other "normal" house in the neighborhood. Through the years, however, walls and rooms that were previously occupied by family pictures and other household pieces quickly converted into a baseball mecca. Our family room was transformed into the "baseball room," filled with one-of-a-kind memorabilia, priceless autographed pictures, and, of course, a big screen television for us to watch countless baseball games. Reading, a passion of both my parents, translated into an ever-growing collection of over three thousand baseball books. Eventually, other than the living room, kitchen, and bathrooms, what started out with one dedicated room for everything baseball blossomed into nearly an entire house of all baseball. The beauty of this restoration to America's pastime was that my mom, Marilyn, was all for it as she, too, had such a passion and love for the game.

My playing career grew, too, beyond my Little League and recreation days to Tarpon Springs High School, home of the Spongers. Despite not playing much in my early high school years, I eventually landed a starting gig on the varsity squad and was an all-district, honorable mention second baseman my senior year. Also, at ages fifteen and sixteen, I was very fortunate to be part of the Upper Pinellas International Baseball club. This team, comprised of local high school players, traveled to Canada and Australia to compete against various teams from both countries. I was also very lucky to have Dan, who traveled with the team as a chaperone, by my side in Australia. Blessed beyond words to have had this opportunity, I remain forever grateful to both my parents for giving it to me.

It didn't really faze me until the summer going into my senior year that I had a shot to possibly play collegiate baseball. Known for my defense, I was an undersized "Punch and Judy" type of hitter who grinded and played the game with tenacity and grit, always looking for ways to help the team. After writing to some smaller D2 and D3 schools, and not getting much attention, I turned my focus to a small private school in Tampa known for their academics, especially in criminology. The other attraction was without a doubt its baseball program as this school had just won back-to-back D2 championships. The University of Tampa is where I finally landed as a walk-on player in the junior varsity program. During my freshman year, I started on the JV team and ultimately got called up to the big squad later in the year where I was used mainly as a defensive replacement late in games. Historically, playing in the shadow of better players, my "3-D philosophy" – determination, desire, and dedication – were the keys that catapulted me to the next level. After working hard that following off-season, I earned a spot on the varsity team, eventually getting the opportunity to start at second base. From my sophomore year on, I was the starting second baseman for one of the most elite D2 programs in the nation. Now, not just known for my glove, gritty play, and selflessness, I matured from a .265 high school hitter to a respectable .300 collegiate hitter. From being that walk-on baseball player to eventually starting three years on a national powerhouse to playing with such elite, unified teams and making it to the D2 World Series in 1996 and 1997, my University of Tampa days will go down as some of the best memories in my life. The University of Tampa not only granted me an opportunity to play college baseball, but also, importantly, it provided me with a top-notch education and the good fortune to meet my future wife, Meg.

Shortly after the 1997 D2 college world series, I was picked up as a free agent by the Johnstown Steal of the Independent Frontier League. What was once a dream finally coming to fruition, I was now playing professional baseball, earning a paycheck, albeit a very small paycheck, and traveling to various cities to play the game I'd always loved. My time in Johnstown, Pennsylvania, came to a scorching halt, however, a few weeks in as one day after a humiliating loss to the Canton Crocodiles, I was called into my manager's office. I'll always remember Hank Manning, skipper for the Steal, sitting me down and telling me I had been traded. What a surreal experience that was – first playing professional baseball, and then, a few weeks into my journey, being told by my manager that I had been traded. Originally, I thought the topic of our conversation was going to be about the dreaded pink slip, but, fortunately, it led to my being traded to the Canton Crocodiles. I recall reading the Johnstown Tribune-Democrat newspaper that next Monday morning and noticing a blurb underneath the headline: *Frontier free fall: Steal tumbles to 1-7 in second half.* Underneath this bold caption read: *Satinoff traded after lopsided home loss.* Wow, reality was kicking in as I packed my bags and headed to Canton, Ohio, where I would later become part of a championship team as the Canton Crocodiles ended up winning the 1997 Frontier League Championship in their inaugural year. I headed back to Canton for spring training in 1998, but, unfortunately, after an arm injury that spring, I got released and my professional baseball career ended.

Meg and I got married in 2001 and soon after parenthood began. We welcomed Ella with open arms into our family in 2004. Two years later Jack was born, and in 2009 William completed the Satinoff family. Throughout my kids' childhoods our national pastime has played such a vital part of our family life. Whether it was watching our kids play softball and baseball for their respective schools and summer leagues or sitting as a family cheering on our household's favorite team, the Tampa Bay Rays, the game of baseball has helped create an even tighter bond for our family. Fortunately, I had the pleasure to coach my daughter when she was a young softball player in Arizona and over the past eight years helped coach William on his travel and Little League teams. I've been very blessed to share my love for the game with my kids, wife, and many others over the years. Gratefully, my family has embraced baseball with the same vigor and passion as I did during my youth. My hope is that my kids will carry on this baseball tradition for generations to come and allow baseball to be a positive influence on their families as it's been on ours.

WHERE IT ALL BEGAN

It was Saturday, August 21, 2021, and our Nolensville, Tennessee, All-Star team had just been defeated by a talented New Hampshire team, 4-1. Two days prior we lost a heartbreaker to Ohio, who ended up losing to Michigan in the U.S. championship game. After the game, I vividly remember circling up near the left field line with coaches, Randy and Chris, and the team. Emotions ran high as the summer to remember had just come to an end. I'll always recall those words Randy said to the boys: "It's okay to be upset because that means you care." And care we did. The 2021 LLWS run was one that I never thought would be surpassed. It's a dream for every young baseball player to make it to the pinnacle of youth sports – Williamsport, Pennsylvania, and the Little League World Series.

The 2021 team was special. It was comprised of five players I'd coached for five to seven years, a few I had coached over the last few years, and others I had never met. I had a strong bond with their parents, siblings, grandparents, and others as friendships grew deep over the years. The manager was Randy Huth, and my fellow assistant coach was Chris Mercado. Both coaches are childhood friends, baseball junkies, and experts in their fields of work, and neither one had a child on the team. When I was asked to help with this team in the fall of 2020, never once did I expect to participate in the journey that we had ahead of us.

Intense rival district games vs. Goodlettsville took place. A state championship in Maryville, Tennessee, was where domination ensued, and homeruns were flying out of the ballpark. Fun times and bonding amongst players and their families took place at a local Drury Inn hotel. A Southeast tournament in Warner Robins, Georgia, was where this group of boys dug deep and were tested to their limit to come back from a heartbreaking defeat by a gritty team out of Georgia. I can still see Nolan Brown throwing that last pitch, Tanner Jackson calling out, "Ball! Ball!" for the pop up, and the whole team running to dog pile – the boys from Nolensville had punched their ticket to the Little League World Series!

Williamsport was a magical place to say the least. Despite going 0-2, the run was epic; the ESPN coverage was unforgettable, and the memories will never be forgotten, especially since the boys wrote in a journal every night from the regional to the world series.

The 2021 LLWS run was simply one of a kind, especially when we made it to the Southeast Regional in Warner Robins. Unfortunately, in 2020 the LLWS was cancelled due to COVID-19. Once regional play started, COVID-19 protocols were put in place to ensure the safety of all players, coaches, and staff members. Every other day each player and coach were required to test for COVID-19. It was a long, drawn-out process as testing took place at the local hotel meeting room we stayed in as a team. Also residing at the local Hampton Inn were the other seven state champions. If one player or coach tested positive, that respective team was automatically eliminated from the tournament. Unfortunately for the team from North Carolina, the virus hit and hit hard. After winning their first game, the boys from North Carolina and their parents had to pack their bags and head home. It was heartbreaking to see boys, coaches, and parents sobbing with tears, walking out of the local hotel thinking about what could have been if it weren't for the pandemic.

When we made it to Williamsport, the COVID-19 protocols didn't end. Every other day, all players and coaches had to do the infamous "spit" COVID-19 test in the dining hall. Fortunately, during the world series, no team was eliminated by the virus; elimination only came from losses on the diamond. Care was an understatement throughout the summer of 2021. We three coaches acted like surrogate dads as we spent 19 straight days with these boys throughout regional and world series play. Because of the dreaded "C" word, the boys couldn't get close to anyone during their stay in the regional and the world series. Not a hug from a parent, a handshake from a spectator, or knucks from an opposing team. Masks were mandated throughout all indoor facilities and always worn by the teams until they reached the dugout. At times I thought I owned stock in Lysol and Purell as we had an arsenal of hand sanitizer, spray, and cleaning wipes. We even had a special mouthwash we used every morning throughout the regional and the world series. Whether it was superstition or helped kill the virus, each player and coach took a swig of it every single morning. The parents of this team entrusted us three coaches with their boys, and we were determined to live up to that trust. It was a long, grueling summer, but I would do it all over again, especially with this group of boys and coaches.

Never in the world series 75-year history had there been a year as unique as 2021. There were no international teams; instead, there were 16 U.S. teams comprised of the top two teams from the eight regions. There was no engagement with opposing players, no parade, no fan-filled stadiums (limit was 500 per game). Despite all these uncontrollable challenges, we didn't let a pandemic get in the way of experiencing a once in a lifetime opportunity. We were one of 16 out of 6,500 Little Leagues nationally to participate in the Little League World Series. We were District 7, Tennessee, Southeast Champions. This team will go down in history as the first Nolensville Little League team to make it to the Little League World Series. These boys helped pave the way for the 2022 team and will always be a part of the Nolensville Little League family.

Nolan "Nolie" Brown, Ryan "Ryno" Newell, Cason "Case" Booher, Hutch "Chicken-man" Weaver, Mateo "The Magnet" Bruzzese, Gabe "Gaber" Shepler, Ryan "The Scientist" Pearson, William "Dreus" Dreussi, Tanner "Tan-Man" Jackson, Drew "Wags" Wagner, Rocco "Roc" Stark, Jack "Jack & Cheese" Rhodes, and William "Sati" Satinoff –THANK YOU for letting me be part of this ride. It was certainly a ride with twists and turns, but a year I will always treasure.

One Team, One Dream.

The 2021 Nolensville Little League World Series Team

THE SPRING OF 2022 – NOLENSVILLE LITTLE LEAGUE REGULAR SEASON

It was a Sunday afternoon at the Nolensville Little League complex (better known as the quad) where the 2022 12u rec evaluations were taking place. Having had the pleasure to coach on the All-Star team last year, I was called on to help with the assessments. Since a Nolensville team had gone to the Little League World Series the year before, one would think the overall Little League attendance would go up and soared it did. There was a 30% increase in overall Little League baseball spring attendance from 2020 to 2021. President of the league, David Jones; VP of Baseball Operations, Blake Bivens; and Bill Packard, VP of Baseball Administration, all volunteers and instrumental to the growth and success of the league, were hard at work ensuring the 2022 spring season got off the ground without a hitch. Having made the LLWS the year prior, both kids and their parents wanted to be part of a potential dynasty. Right from the start there were brief evaluations that consisted of a few ground and fly balls in right field, five swings, and five pitches thrown by the pitchers. It was a very basic skills evaluation to determine where everyone measured up going into the annual managers' draft.

Following the players' evaluation, the 12u draft took place where managers from all seven teams gathered in the quad's press box and drafted their 2022 spring teams. Randy Huth was managing the Braves again, and David Jones and I were assisting him as coaches. As in previous years, any of the coaches' kids were automatically on that team. Parents could also request that their child be on a specific team or with a particular coach. That said, there were numerous parent requests for their player to be on the Braves with Randy. The good news is that we were able to accommodate most, if not all, the requests in 2022. Joining Randy, David and me, were my son, William, and Patrick (David's youngest son) along with 2021 LLWS catcher, Jack Rhodes. One of Jack's Franklin Bomber teammates, Caz Logue, wanted to play Little League in 2022 and joined our Braves team as well. Another player that had requested to be on the team due to a connection with David Jones was a local Nolensville kid by the name of JF Forni. We also had two 2021 LLWS players' siblings on our team with Gideon Shepler, younger brother of Gabe Shepler, and Liam Bruzzese, younger brother of Mateo Bruzzese, joining the squad. All in all, Randy did a terrific job putting together a great group of kids looking to have fun and improve their game. Coming off a 2021 12u Little League rec title, the expectations were, hopefully, to make it back-to- back.

Throughout March our team held numerous practices at the Nolensville quad all in preparation for our opening day matchup with the Padres. This opening day was going to be like no other opening day in Nolensville Little League history. On Friday, April 1st , the league was going to honor our 2021 LLWS team, introduce all the baseball teams from t-ball to 14u, and to cap it off, our Braves team was going to play the Padres in the first spring game of the year. The atmosphere was electric as there were well over 1,000 moms, dads, siblings, players, and fans that congregated around field #2 at the Little League complex. It was such a beautiful spring evening to honor a special group of kids that put Nolensville Little League on the map. As each team was introduced by Blake Bivens, the boys (especially the younger ones) would trot from the right field line with their team down the first base line, crossing home plate while parents and fans gave a rousing round of applause. What a thrill for these youngsters as they were the stars of the night for that brief, but very cool, introduction. I'll always remember the hands-on interaction our 2021 LLWS team had with the younger players. Not only high fives and knucks were going down, but also our LLWS team made a tunnel with their hands held high for the younger players to run through. There were smiles, laughs, and elation amongst our LLWS players and Little Leaguers hoping one day to emulate them. Tons of proud parents gravitated to the backstop fence trying to get the best possible picture of their favorite player. Finally, the time had come when our 2021 LLWS team took the stage and were honored in front of the cheerful crowd. One by one, the players and coaches were introduced and received a standing ovation.

Following the introduction, Chris Mercado (three-time LLWS coach), who was stepping down in 2022 to spend more time with his boys, threw out the ceremonial first pitch. However, there was one more surprise for the 2021 team. Behind field #2, bolted to the brown and tan stones of the concession stand, rested a commemorative plaque with all the players' and coaches' names that would be displayed forever at the Little League complex. Now, the time had come; the festivities had ended, and our first Braves rec game was set to begin. At that April 1st, first rec game of the season, little did I imagine what was in store for the rest of the summer.

The Braves 12u regular season was so enjoyable. Three team rules that were instilled by Coach Randy from the start were (1) have fun, (2) continue to improve, (3) hustle. Our team ended up 9-4, with our only losses to the Dodgers and Mets. It was a very gratifying season as the Braves took the 12u championship for the second consecutive year. Most importantly, the kids had loads of fun, continued to improve on their skillsets, and showed a ton of hustle and passion when stepping onto the diamond.

THE ASSEMBLY OF ALL-STARS

Going into the 2022 spring Little League season, Randy and I knew we had two players automatically making this year's all-star team. Returnees William Satinoff and Jack Rhodes were locks on the team since they were both the only 11-year-olds from the 2021 LLWS team. Assembling the rest of the team would be challenging as we recognized some players from the seven Little League teams, but there were others that we surely didn't. From the initial spring evaluations and forward through the regular season, Randy and I were like hawks at the ballpark. We not only coached our Braves team, but also, importantly, kept a keen eye on other players from the remaining teams.

We consistently talked before, during, and after games about the "who's who" on the other teams. Of course, there was a lot of feedback given to us from the other coaches about whom they recommended keeping an eye on as well. The conversations between Randy and me had been constant, whether it was at the fields, on the phone, or even during post-game dinners. One thing was for sure; we had 11 remaining spots and a ton of talent to gauge. As the regular season came to an end, each head coach nominated several kids from his team to be part of the all-star selection process. Some teams nominated two kids while others nominated three or even four. Each of the seven teams had nominees that moved forward to the all-star selection process.

It was now GO time! We had very little time to pick our all-star team. During our selection process, we did various drills to better evaluate the 31 kids that were trying to make a lasting impression and get selected to the 2022 Nolensville Little League All-Star team. One of the biggest tests was having the players face live pitching from several of last year's players during intersquad games. Despite these pitchers being a year older, Randy and I wanted to push these potential all-stars to the limit since we'd probably face this type of elite pitching vs. our arch-rivals in Goodlettsville during district play. These all-star nominees worked hard, showed tremendous grit, and competed, knowing only 11 spots were on the line. All these kids were super talented, and we knew each of them would represent Nolensville Little League with pride. However, there were only 11 spots remaining, and, unfortunately, we knew there would be some disappointed kids and parents when tryouts concluded. However, the time had come, and after much deliberation, Randy and I narrowed down our final 13 players. Following one last dinner and discussion at one of our favorite local restaurants, Cabo's, Randy sent out the communication email to the parents of the 31 players listing the kids that made the 2022 Nolensville Little League All-Star team. Suffice it to say, emotions were high with both joy and disappointment, but we were confident in the final decisions we had made and were proud to present our 2022 Nolensville Little League All-Stars:

William "Sati" Satinoff, Jack "Jack & Cheese" Rhodes, Wright "Wrighty" Martin, Trent "T-Rex" McNiel, Drew "Drewbie/Mountain Drew" Chadwick, Lane "Lane-O" Dever, Caz "Cazzy" Logue, Charlie "Chuck Diesel" Malom, Bo "Bo-Bo" Daniel, JF Forni, Josiah "Jo-Jo/Big Hand Joe" Porter, Nash "Nasher" Carter, and Grayson "Mullet Man" May.

There were 11 Little League 12-year-old players selected and two true 11-year-olds. There was a method to the madness in selecting two 11-year-olds. Last year, both William and Jack were the two 11-year-olds on the team. Randy liked having two 11-year-olds as the experience factor played a major role on the following year's team. This year those players were Nash and Grayson, who were not only 11, but also, both very deserving from a talent standpoint.

Now that the team was selected, we had a lot of work to get done both on and off the field. Our next step was determining who was going to be our third coach. Throughout the year Randy and I went back and forth on who we thought would be the right fit. In 2021, I was asked to become the third coach. I knew of Chris Mercado from his Music City baseball days but didn't know Randy at all. We were in a similar situation in 2022 as Randy and I knew of a few of the other coaches but didn't have a really strong relationship with any of them.

In the middle of the year, we identified a potential candidate. We had heard from others that the Dodgers head coach, Mark Carter, was a phenomenal coach who was great with kids and had very strong character. After assembling the team, Randy approached Mark with the "ask." I remember telling Randy if the coach he asked showed any sign of hesitancy, we would need to immediately pass. Knowing the grind that we experienced in 2021, I was certain we needed someone who was 100% committed and passionate as the road to Williamsport was grueling. Fortunately, Mark enthusiastically accepted, and we welcomed Lincoln County native, Mark Carter, the Dodger's head coach, Senior Associate Athletic Director at Vanderbilt University, baseball junkie, and just all-around great dude to our staff. Little did I know, then, just how much Mark was going to leave such a lasting impression on our team, our coaches, and our Little League family.

EXPECTATIONS, PREPARATION, AND UNITY

Now that the team was constructed, we had to have our first parents' meeting. I recall this meeting from last year when Randy was very frank and open with the parents about expectations. Except for my family, the Rhodeses, the Logues, and the Fornis (from the Braves), nobody really knew Randy Huth. Some parents may have casually talked to him during the year, said hello to him while at the fields, or just knew of him through conversation. Nevertheless, after a brief introduction of the coaches, Randy drew the line in the sand and told the parents that there were going to be decisions they wouldn't agree with. He followed up by saying there were going to be things that he would get wrong. However, at the end of the day, the parents needed to trust him and the process.

During our first practice, Randy sat the team down and set expectations with them. His conversation was short and to the point as he looked each player in the eye. Each of these kids was the superstar on his respective team. Many of them batted 4th, played shortstop, and were the aces of the staff. Randy made it clear to them that there is no "I" when it comes to this Nolensville Little League All-Star team. He proceeded to say that their roles may be a lot different than what they had done on past teams. He also made it clear that there may be times when they wouldn't play the field or would only get one at bat. He asked the boys if they understood. Following his question came an emphatic shake of the head from each of the boys. If this team was going to be successful, like last year's LLWS team, every player would need to know his role because all individual egos were thrown out the door when it came to the Nolensville Little League All-Stars and the road to Williamsport.

Following the communication of who made this year's all-star team on June 2nd, a message was sent out to the parents from Randy, outlining what was ahead for the team in terms of practices and games. We had fewer than three weeks to prepare as a newly formed squad. The District 7 tournament was circled on the calendar starting June 21st, and Nolensville was hosting the tournament this year.

As practices got longer in the Tennessee summer heat, so did our team's determination and resiliency to keep working and improving as one. From bunt coverages, to first and third defenses, to situations, to "chaos" and "last resort" drills, our defense was shaping up. With batting practice on the field and more in the cages, the kids' swings got crisper, and balls were jumping off the bat. Also, knowing the importance of baserunning, we consistently worked on our turns, extending singles to doubles, delayed steals, and even the infamous fall-down play. In bullpen after bullpen, our pitchers ramped up their stamina and constantly worked on throwing strikes. One thing was sure; we would need to win the freebie war if we wanted to win district and keep advancing. The freebie war in baseball terms meant no walks by our pitchers and no errors by our defense.

Before every game, each team would do an infield set, better known as infield/outfield. Randy, whose dad coached Tennessee Little League baseball for 40+ years, wanted to honor his dad by incorporating a unique infield set for this year's team. The story has it that there was a team that Randy's dad, Jim, coached years ago that just had a hard time fielding balls during their infield set, so instead of using a ball during the infield set, Jim would take a swing with his bat with no ball. It made the team focus on their fundamentals and added some extra fun to this pre-game routine. During that year's all-star campaign, spectators would crowd the stands just to watch the team's infield set as it was certainly one of a kind. Fast forward to 2022, Randy implemented this one-of-a-kind, pre-game tradition, and like anything else, we practiced it until it was sharp with no flaws. Better known as phantom infield or, back in the day, as shadow ball, Randy would toss the imaginary ball as I knocked two fungo bats together making the sound of the ball hitting the bat.

In terms of baseball readiness, we were very close to being in total game mode. Even more important than the physical part of the game was the mental side and how this newly formed group of boys would coexist. Fortunately, there were pockets of boys that had played together on other teams. Although this certainly helped with the cohesiveness, it was the boys themselves and their one common-goal mindset to get to Williamsport that proved to be the X-factor. The coaches noticed a bond like no other from the outset. Kids not knowing each other that well started to act like kids that were teammates for years. What certainly helped pave the way was the leadership of two players that made it to the LLWS the year before: William and Jack. Known as the "veterans" of the team, many of the kids looked up to these two boys. As 11-year-olds, they experienced what most kids never get to experience. These two vets learned how to be leaders from many of the kids from the 2021 team – none more so than 2021 superstar, Nolan Brown. His leadership in 2021 was critical to the success and camaraderie of that team. The love for each other was forming in front of our eyes.

Our first test was soon approaching as we had multiple exhibition games against other all-star teams around the state and even from Kentucky. Later in June, we headed up to Clarksville and had a double header with the Clarksville National All-Star team. The boys from Nolensville did not disappoint as we took the double header while putting up 31 runs and only allowing two. As practices resumed following that doubleheader win, we continued to evaluate our team and worked on developmental opportunities. Following the Clarksville National games, we played Warren County in another double header, this time at our place. The hits just kept coming, and we continued to play sound baseball. The last exhibition games we played before districts were against Bowling Green East. I remember the coaches saying how this would be a true test as Bowling Green East was managed by legendary Little League coach, Rick Kelley. Historically, they've had powerhouse teams, making it to the LLWS on three separate occasions. We took the 1.5-hour drive up Interstate 65 to Bowling Green, Kentucky, and played them in a double header. Both games were dog fights, and the caliber of play was the highest we'd faced to date. After two long, hard fought games, we ended a long night with two more wins, 11-4 and 10-7. The 2022 Nolensville Little League All-Star team was ready. Our families, who had shown an extraordinary amount of support to date, were ready. Our Little League, our town, and our fans were all ready to bring on districts!

DISTRICT 7 CHAMPIONSHIP - A RIVALRY FOR THE AGES

The moment had come, and Nolensville Little League was about to host districts. The league had never hosted a district tournament, so we knew this would be a memorable occasion for our league, team, and community. The 12u District 7 is made up of four leagues: Nolensville, Goodlettsville, Murfreesboro, and McCabe. The honor to host districts rotates from league to league each year; Murfreesboro had the pleasure of hosting the tournament in 2021. In the last 11 years, South Nashville Little League or Nolensville Little League has won six District 7 titles (2013, 2014, 2015, 2018, 2021 and 2022). In 2013 and 2014, Chris Mercado managed the South Nashville teams that made it back-to-back to the Little League World Series. Every other year since 2011, Goodlettsville has won the District 7 championship (2011, 2012, 2016, 2017 and 2019). I had always heard of the South Nashville/Nolensville rivalry with Goodlettsville, but never really put two and two together until last year during our district tournament. There were stories about the intense rivalries one would hear about at the ballpark or while reminiscing about the history of middle Tennessee Little League. In fact, when people think of Little League in Tennessee, the first thing that comes to mind is the deep history between Goodlettsville and South Nashville/Nolensville. In the last 11 years one of these two programs had made it to the Southeast Regional, representing the state of Tennessee. There was a lot on the line in 2022 as Good-lettsville was looking for some revenge, and the Nolensville Little League All-Stars were looking to get back to the Tennessee State Championship and make another run at Williamsport.

Prior to the district tournament last year, we had a team dinner at one of the local Nolensville restaurants, Wings to Go. To keep the tradition going, we decided to venture down to Wings to Go again following our last practice on the Friday before district play. The restaurant was filled with a sea of black and gold as our players, coaches, parents, and siblings packed Wings to Go for some great food, and, hopefully, inspiration. In preparation for the biggest tournament most of these kids would ever play, we decided to ask the 2021 team to give some motivational words of wisdom to the team. As we finished our dinner and played the encouraging messages from last year's LLWS team, I could only think back to the magical time we had together making the run to Williamsport last year. Everyone heard passion, motivation, and sincerity as each player gave his short, but powerful, pep talk. There was a common theme coming across each of the 2021 LLWS player's messages. The constant words of "Beat Goodlettsville" echoed throughout the air as eyes were glued on the big screen television mounted on the side wall of the restaurant. As the night ended, the coaching staff reminded the boys to get a good night's sleep and to cherish the moments as the journey to Williamsport would begin in less than 24 hours.

Saturday, June 25th

Our Nolensville Little League team was about to take the field for the first time in the post season against McCabe Little League. Our team's mantra was "One Team, One Dream." It was the slogan we used with the 2021 team, so initially we thought what better words describe this team and this journey we were about to take. Those four words brought such good luck and karma to the boys of summer last year, we wanted to repeat it. The "One Team" was simple. Every player on the team had a role. Big or small... it didn't matter because if we were going to make it back to the LLWS, every player would be contributing in one way or another. "One Dream" symbolized the dream to make it to the LLWS in Williamsport, Pennsylvania. Our goal last year was to get to the pinnacle, and it started the same way for this special group of boys in 2022.

A tradition that carried over before each game from last year was to have the players and coaches gently touch a good luck hat that was displayed in the dugout at every game. This special hat, filled with at least 75+ Little League pins gathered throughout the years, was in dedication of Randy's dad, Jim, who, unfortunately, passed away in 2018. A legendary Little League coach from Clarksville, Tennessee, Jim Huth's spirit shone brightly during each and every game throughout our LLWS run.

Randy with his dad's legendary good luck hat

Once the game started, we got out of the gates quickly during district play as our bats put up 16 runs, and we limited McCabe Little League to two runs. It was a 16-2 final in four innings due to the Little League run rule. Jack Rhodes and

Bo Daniel hit big flies, Nash Carter pitched three strong innings, and William Satinoff closed out the game. Despite the first big win in districts, we all knew who would be awaiting us in the next round: Goodlettsville Little League, the boys 45 minutes north of us who took care of business by beating Murfreesboro the game before.

Sunday, June 26th

It was a hot summer night as Nolensville Little League was about to go head-to-head with our arch-rival, Goodlettsville Little League. Our coaching staff knew how intense this game would be and that not just the physical preparation, but also the mental preparation of our team would be pivotal. I recall the pre-game huddle Randy and the coaches had with the team, explaining to our boys that this game would be the biggest game in their lives. Not only because of the rivalry, but also because Nolensville was hosting, and we recognized the crowd would be electric on both sides.

Rewinding from a year ago at districts in Murfreesboro, my mind went to the two games we played against Goodlettsville, which were like a post-season battle between bitter rivals, such as the Yankees vs. Red Sox or the Dodgers vs. Giants. The Goodlettsville fans from last year came out strong and a bit over-zealous. Their cow bells rang loudly and so was their intensity. Knowing what we knew from last year, we not only prepared our team with what could possibly go on, but, importantly, we informed our fans and town that it was a must that they bring the noise when our two teams squared off.

The boys from Nolensville came out swinging right from the get-go as Bo Daniel hit a towering grand slam in the first inning to give Nolensville a 4-0 lead after the first. Our crowd, dressed in black and gold, erupted with applause. Chills went down my spine seeing the hundreds and hundreds of fans cheering on Nolensville when Bo hit that grand slam to put us on the board. In the second, Goodlettsville brought in its ace who was pumping 70 MPH fireballs from 46 feet. Goodlettsville came back and put up a run in the third and three more in the top of the fifth. Goodlettsville's ace had shut our offense down until the bottom of the sixth inning when pure drama unfolded; the electricity from our crowd erupted throughout the streets of Nolensville. Drew Chadwick stepped up to the plate in the bottom of the sixth with one out and runners on first and third. On a 1-0 count, Drew launched a towering fly ball just over the reach of the right fielder scoring Charlie Malom with the game-winning run. Pandemonium ensued as the bench stormed the field to congratulate both Charlie and Drew. This victory was a big one as the tournament was a double elimination tournament, and we knew for Goodlettsville to advance they'd have to beat us twice at our home park. The hitting stars for the night were clearly Bo and Drew. Trent McNiel threw 2 2/3 innings of one-run ball, Drew Chadwick came in for some middle relief, and Jack Rhodes closed the door with five K's in 1 2/3 innings of work to collect the save.

Tuesday, June 28th

After much celebrating with the team, family, and fans we had to collect ourselves since we knew the job was not over. With a day's rest, we took on Goodlettsville again. We decided to start an hour earlier due to no other games being played and to alleviate some of the direct sunlight into the batter's box as there were visibility challenges throughout the year. There was no question who we were looking to start on the bump for this potential district clinching game – none other than Jack & Cheese. The coaches knew this tall, slender, and savvy veteran was the right choice as Jack had dominated Goodlettsville in the first game and only threw 30 pitches that game. The game went back and forth as the offenses from both teams came out strong. Who would have thought another nail-biting game would come down to one run and another thrilling finish?

Going into the top of the sixth, Nolensville was down 5-4. Up came pinch hitter, JF Forni, to lead off the top of the sixth. With a crowd of 500+ Nolensville faithful going crazy, Forni stepped into one and hit a scorching ground ball to the shortstop and legged out an infield hit. I remember thinking if we got our leadoff guy on, this game was going to end in our favor. Two consecutive outs transpired after JF led off with his base hit. Now with two outs, top of the sixth and a runner on first, William came to the plate. The chants of "Sati! Sati!" echoed throughout the Nolensville night. On a 1-0 count, Sati hit a clutch line drive down the right field line bringing Forni to third base. It was now two outs, men on second and third, and Wright Martin coming to the plate. Wright Martin, one of the most gifted and biggest athletes on the field, was poised to keep the inning going. As the "Sati-Daddy" chants continued, I called our offensive timeout. In Little League baseball, during each offensive inning, a team can call a timeout. I remember Randy always telling me to make sure we use these timeouts, but only in situations when we really needed to speak to a player. Well, let's just say the time was right to give a little pep talk to the gentle giant, Wright. On a 1-1 count, Wrighty hit a little dribbler down the third base line and came through with an infield single. It was now bases loaded with two outs for #12, Jack Rhodes. First pitch swinging, Rhodes turned on a curve ball and hit a hard ground ball down the line past the sprawling first baseman scoring JF and William. The crowd, who had waited patiently through a lengthy lightning delay, was absolutely going nuts. This special group of players just rallied together and came up with some clutch performances to give the team the lead. As fireworks prematurely exploded in the air behind the right field fence (courtesy of LLWS alum Hutch Weaver's dad, Brandon) the inning continued as Daniel stepped to the plate. Bo hit a ground ball between the 5 and 6-hole scoring Martin, but as Rhodes tried to score, a rock-solid throw from the left fielder nailed Jack for the third out. The top of the sixth inning was one to remember and finally ended, but not before the Nolensville Little League had rallied with two outs to take a 7-5 lead.

The squad was pumped; the song "Black and Yellow" (the 2021 theme song) was playing loudly through the speakers, and Drew Chadwick was about to come back out in the bottom of the 6th to potentially close out the game. After a leadoff walk, a flyout, and a wild pitch, a Goodlettsville player stood on second base with one out. We were two outs away from capturing back-to-back District 7 championships, but nobody said it would be easy, nor one heck of a finish. With a man on second, Chadwick unleashed a wild pitch, and the runner from second hustled home to make the score 7-6 Nolensville. At the plate, Bo couldn't find the baseball, and when he did, it was a bang-bang play. Even after Randy came out to question the safe call, and the umps had a brief huddle, it remained 7-6

Nolensville, now with one out. Suddenly, the Nolensville crowd became quieter as the Goodlettsville fans became louder and more confident. The next batter for Goodlettsville got on by a walk and was the tying run. The Goodlettsville dugout erupted as all the momentum was shifting its way. After a bloop single to center, it was now first and second with one out for Goodlettsville, and the nerves around the stadium were on edge, especially for the Nolensville fans. On a 1-1 count, Drew Chadwick induced a 4-6-3 double play as it went Carter to Satinoff to Martin ending the game and, ultimately, giving the Nolensville Little League All-Star team another District 7 championship.

As more fireworks exploded over the tree line in right field, our boys were filled with joy and gloves were being tossed in the air with excitement. Fans proceeded to rush the field; hugs and high fives were overflowing, and at the end a centerfold picture was taken of the team holding up the number "1" as they were, proudly, District 7 champions.

2022 District 7 Champions

As I look back and reminisce, everything about our district tournament was miraculous. From the electric crowd's sea of black and gold apparel to Brandon Porter's incredible play-by-play announcing, and Ingle Martin's between-innings deejaying those renowned songs, to just plain and simple outstanding youth baseball and teamwork by so many talented young men – there was no other word but miraculous to describe it. Many players, parents, and fans to this day say that the Nolensville vs. Goodlettsville battles were some of the best games they'd ever witnessed. Looking back (literally, as I've watched these games on video) I'd have to agree. It was another super proud moment for our coaches, kids, families, league, and fans as our road to Williamsport started to become more of a reality.

As the emotional high of winning the district championship started to come to an end, our team knew we still had a long way to go to ultimately get to Williamsport and the LLWS. Next up was preparing for the Tennessee State Championship, which would consist of the top eight teams representing their respective districts. Last year the state tournament was hosted in Maryville, Tennessee, about a three-hour drive from Nolensville. Fortunately, this year the state tournament would only be 45 minutes south of Nolensville in Goodletts-ville. Having the tournament in Goodlettsville meant a few positive things for our team. One, the boys would be able to sleep in their own homes and in their own beds. Secondly, and probably most importantly, we knew the fan turnout to see the team play would be strong as the fan support throughout district play was simply amazing.

There was a long three-week window between when we ended district play to the beginning of the state tournament. We went through the same timeline last year, so we were prepared on what we needed to do to keep the boys baseball ready, loose, and, most importantly, focused on what was in store for them in the weeks to come. We continued to practice hard during the week as weekends were a time for rest. Always looking to improve our game and get real game situations in, we had some of the boys from last year's team come back and throw live to our hitters. It was not only great to get in live hitting from experienced players, but also to have those players from last year's team around our boys provided a sense of confidence for our team. The relationships both Randy Huth and Chris Mercado had with so many Little Leagues across Tennessee, Kentucky, and Ohio, enabled us to network across different Little Leagues and schedule exhibition games. Like we had prepared for the district tournament, we also wanted to incorporate exhibi-tion games vs. other Little League teams. We were lucky to have the Eastern Little

League All-Stars travel down from Lexington, Kentucky, to play two exhibition games against us. The first exhibition game we played against Eastern Little League resulted in a 10-5 loss. This was our first loss of the summer as every exhibition game prior and throughout district play, we were undefeated. I remember Mark, Randy and me talking about how this loss could be a good thing. It would test our boys to see how they would respond after a defeat. Despite being an exhibition game, the boys rallied together and played much improved baseball capturing a 9-6 win over a very talented Eastern team.

A week following our doubleheader vs. Eastern Little League we traveled up I-40 to play the Smith County Little League All-Stars who would also be playing a few days later in the Tennessee State Championship in Goodlettsville. With timely hitting and strong pitching, our team pulled off a double header sweep. As we played these four exhibition games before the state tournament, the goal was to continue to win and keep some positive momentum, but, even more, it was to keep these boys fresh and game ready in preparation for the state tournament.

The night before the state tournament began, the McNiels hosted a team party at their barn. Not only did our Little League family have a delicious meal catered by Charcoal Cowboy barbeque and watch a baseball classic, "Field of Dreams," but also, we shared a night of great fun and unforgettable moments under the stars.

A COMEBACK FOR THE CENTURIES – THE TN STATE TOURNAMENT

Saturday, July 16th

The state tournament in Goodlettsville was upon us. It was a long, anxious three weeks between our District 7 Championship and the opening day ceremonies for state. Since our Nolensville Little League All-Star team made a trip to Williamsport last year, this year's team certainly had a target on its back. We were the favorites from the start, and we marched into Goodlettsville with some swagger; we were prepared. The state championship started off with team introductions as each district with its flag was introduced that afternoon. There were a lot of competitive juices flowing that afternoon as all eight teams scoped out the competition as each team was introduced. As the District 7 champions from Nolensville were introduced, loud applause erupted, and our team headed from the back edge of the infield dirt to the pitcher's mound to have our picture taken.

As the afternoon grew longer, so did our excitement; this team was ready to take on our first opponent in the Lexington Little League All-Star team at 7:00 p.m. Our first game vs. Lexington was a shortened game as the boys from

Nolensville put on a hitting and pitching clinic and shut out Lexington 12-0. William Satinoff hit an inside the park homerun and was one of three players, along with Trent McNiel and Nash Carter, with multiple hits. Trent, Nash, and Caz threw a combined shutout giving up only four hits, one walk, and striking out five. A convincing "W" for Nolensville began their quest to capture the state championship.

However, there was no time for rest following our victory over Lexington Little League as we were taking on Columbia American Little League on Sunday at 3:00 p.m. A bit of a secondary rival to Goodlettsville had developed between Columbia and Nolensville after Nolensville beat Columbia 9-4 during last year's state championship competition. This Little League, 30 miles southwest of Nolensville, also had some history winning the Tennessee State Championship as they had won back-to-back titles in 2005 and 2006. We had a thorough scouting report of their team as two of our dads (Dino Rhodes and John Logue) watched their team play against Eastern Little League (Lexington, Kentucky) when they, too, played an exhibition double header. The Columbia team had some strong hitters and were deep in pitching. We knew this would be a big test for our squad.

Sunday, July 17th

Like the first game of the state tournament vs. Lexington, we had an awesome crowd from Nolensville come out to support the boys. It was a pitching duel from the start as our ace, Jack Rhodes, kept their bats silent, tossing four scoreless innings while only giving up two hits and punching out seven batters. Columbia's pitching staff went head-to-head with us, stifling our bats while also silencing our loud, but respectful, crowd. Then, in the bottom of the fifth inning, the scoreless tie was no more as Columbia rallied putting together some consecutive base hits that led to three runs on the board.

Going into the top of the sixth inning our boys were a bit dazed, but we were still confident we had the resiliency to come back. After Jack Rhodes got on by an error and Bo Daniel followed up with a hard single to left field, Drew Chadwick came up clutch and singled to the second baseman scoring Rhodes. Unfortunately, the final score ended up not in our favor as we lost to Columbia 3-1. Plain and simple, Columbia's pitching dominated from start to finish. From their ace, who started the game, to their Little League 11-year-old phenom who came in relief and threw 2 2/3 innings of two-hit ball while striking out five of our batters, they were the better baseball team on that given Sunday.

Following the game, when we huddled down the right field line, the coaches could see and feel the agony of defeat in our players' eyes. None of us expected to lose that game. Coaches, players, fans, and spectators fully thought we'd have a victory coming out of that Columbia game, but there was no time to hang our heads and sulk. It was the coaches' job to pick these boys up and get them ready for what would be a huge challenge coming out of the losers' bracket. As Randy's post-game speech concluded, we could feel a bit of melancholy surrounding the outside of our dugout where parents and fans patiently waited for the team. Columbia walked off the field with their heads high, glowing with confidence, as they had just defeated Nolensville Little League, the perennial powerhouse who had just made it to the LLWS the year before. The staggering loss to Columbia served as one of the biggest motivational times of the summer for this team as what was about to unfold was going to be a run for the ages for this determined Nolensville Little League All-Star team.

Following the tough loss to Columbia, the boys and their families headed back home to get a good night's sleep. There was certainly no rest for the weary as we knew to become state champions again, we'd have to tally up five consecutive wins – two straight against Columbia Little League as they were undefeated in state play. However, right now, there was only one thing on our minds and that was a Monday night elimination game against Maryville Little League. Prior to every game at the state championship, we would meet near a big tree at Moss Wright Park in Goodlettsville where the state championship was being played. Before we broke for batting practice, Randy would gather up the boys, talk through our pre-game preparation, and provide some motivational words of wisdom. Needless to say, the challenge this team was about to encounter would be the biggest test to date.

Monday, July 18th

Up until the Columbia loss, our team's mantra was "One Team, One Dream." I clearly remember Randy huddling up the team the day of the Maryville game and, vigorously, saying to the boys that we would no longer say, "One Team, One Dream." Despite using this rally cry since the start of last year's run, the rationale was that "One Team, One Dream" belonged to the 2021 team. Randy also thought change was needed, especially coming off the heartbreak loss to Columbia the night before and bringing on a new team saying seemed to be the answer. From that game forward our team was all about belief. Belief that we could rebound from a colossal loss. Belief that this team, collectively, could not only come back and win the state championship, bring home the Southeast Regional title, and make it to Williamsport, but also, even more notably, make a run and win the 2022 Little League World Series. However, we also knew the importance of winning one inning at a time and not looking ahead to any future games. "We Believe." This was our new identity. Every time we huddled up, it was shouted from the mountaintops: "We What? We Believe!" Never did I think these two words of "We Believe" would have such a monumental impact on not just our players and coaches, but also, essentially, with our fans and community, too.

Although I've never been a very big superstitious guy, I think the baseball gods were telling me to do something a little different for myself as well as for the team after the Columbia loss. During pre-game batting practice, I always wore an undershirt as I knew I would get a bit sweaty during the 45-minute BP session. For the pre-game BP against Maryville, I decided to change things up and wear my blue and red Nolensville Little League dry-fit t-shirt. Little did I know that t-shirt would get a lot of great use for the rest of the summer. For the team, I decided to bring some pre-game sugar. Following the national anthem and starting lineups, I would go into my backpack and unveil one of my all-time favorite candies, Mike & Ike. Now, it wasn't like every player on the team flocked to my box of Mike & Ike, but most kids gathered around as I dumped a few pieces into their snatching hands. Some players only wanted one, others had to have three, and some would take the entire box if they could. Apparently, a little superstition was budding among some of them, too.

As the next game was about to begin, T-Rex took the mound vs. Maryville. After a scoreless top of the first inning, our bats started off hot as the boys put up three runs in the first followed by another five runs in the bottom of the second. Coming off a one-run performance the night before, it was a huge confidence builder to put up an eight spot after two innings. Nash Carter came in relief for Trent and shut down the team from Maryville, and we ended up winning in four innings by the score of 11-1. It was another tremendous pitching performance from the Trent and Nash duo. Nash also was a machine getting on base as he scored four times. Jack & Cheese and Sati had multi-hit games, and Jack and Drew Chadwick each drove in three runs. It was a win-or-go-home scenario for our team. Putting up an 11 spot certainly helped gain back our confidence with our bats after being shut down by Columbia the night before. One down and four to go. We knew what was still ahead of us and understood the importance of not looking onward, but taking one game, one inning, and one AB at a time. Next up was a rematch vs. Lexington Little League. We Believe.

Tuesday, July 19th

Prior to our rematch vs. Lexington Little League, we had a bit of a surprise for the boys. Last year our state championship was played in Maryville, Tennessee. It was a three-hour drive from the Nolensville area, so the boys and their families had an opportunity to stay together at a local Drury Inn 20 minutes down the road in Knoxville. The time the boys and their families had together at the hotel was so memorable. From swimming in the pool to hotel tag to eating together at the local Chipotle, the bonding that took place not only cemented friendships forever, but also helped build camaraderie that affected the entire team throughout our Little League World Series run. Knowing that we weren't going to stay at a local hotel in Goodlettsville because of the short 45-minute commute, we decided to surprise the boys with a cabin for two nights outside of Goodlettsville. The team understood, though, that the only way we were going to spend two priceless nights of fun and laughter was if we continued to win baseball games.

On game day the boys from Nolensville and their families trekked 45 minutes up I-65 to Moss Wright Park for a rematch against Lexington Little League. Not only were the parents' vehicles packed with their sons' baseball gear, but also with two days' worth of luggage for a potential stay at the fun-filled cabin.

Luckily, it was another beautiful evening filled with a whole lot of passionate Nolensville fans. The offense started off hot once again as Drew Chadwick went big fly in the top of the first inning to give Nolensville a quick 3-0 lead. The second inning brought more offense as two more runs crossed the plate. Chadwick was on the bump again and hurled two scoreless innings before giving up two runs in the third. After a back-and-forth offensive performance by both teams, we were able to close the door and come away with a 10-7 victory. It was another multi-hit performance by the two veterans, Satinoff and Rhodes, and Chadwick and Satinoff each had 4 RBIs to lead the offense. We used five pitchers (Chadwick, Logue, Satinoff, May, and Daniel) to finish off Lexington. It was especially exciting to see Grayson May on the mound as it was the first time in the post season that he had thrown off the mound. Grayson had been sidelined for months with an arm injury, so this was definitely a confidence builder for the young lefty. After our post-game talk, the boys came off the field with joy and a ton of excitement as they knew a beautiful, empty cabin was awaiting them. Two down and three to go. We Believe.

When Randy threw out the idea to Mark and me about having the boys stay at a cabin, I immediately thought who in the heck would be the ones supervising thirteen 11–12-year-olds in a remote cabin tucked away in the woods outside Goodlettsville, Tennessee, for two nights. Simple. . . the three coaches. One by one cars drove up the winding driveway to the awaiting cabin. Boys scurried from their parents' vehicles and were welcomed by a refrigerator and closet full of every type of snack imaginable, an array of drinks, and even some healthy food like watermelon and strawberries. The cabin, which had three levels, was the perfect get-away for 13 boys looking to have fun and build memories with each other. From the moment the boys ran through the back door, they sprinted up the flight of stairs to be welcomed by two separate bedrooms. Beds were called and bags were tossed by the side. Right from the beginning we could tell the time we'd spend together would be unforgettable. Playing pool and arcade games to lounging in the outdoor hot tub the fun was just getting started. After dinner, there were showers and some more laughter as lights out was soon approaching. Despite all the fun and enjoyment taking place, we knew we had more business to take care of as the following night we were going to face Daniel Boone Little League in another elimination game. Curfew was set, the lights were dimmed, and the boys and three coaches headed to bed in preparation for another big win.

We let the boys sleep in a little following the first night at the cabin. Once awake, we all headed down to the main level of the cabin to enjoy a team breakfast. We had some down time before we had to head to the field for our pre-game batting practice and warm-ups. The goal was to keep the team loose, so we decided to just hang out at the cabin and let the boys enjoy their time together. Last year during our LLWS run, the coaches did a lot of videotaping. Whether it was videoing the boys practicing their interviewing skills or asking what they've enjoyed most about the experience, I knew having footage throughout the journey would be priceless for the parents and, eventually, for the players. That said, it was time for some reflection time. For the next hour, it was going to be quiet time around the cabin as the boys visualized what they were going to do to help bring Nolensville another victory later that night. Then, using my iPhone, I videotaped each boy while he talked about his reflection time. After an hour of the team reflecting on the upcoming game, I was super curious to hear what they had to say. Not surprisingly, all their comments had two common themes: thoughts of how each player was going to help the team win and how each would be a good teammate. This was simply invaluable commentary from this group of young men. Uploaded on my iPhone were videos that would be shared with their parents, and, hopefully, these innocent voices would be replayed years down the road, reflecting on some of the greatest times of their childhoods. One thing was for sure coming out of that reflection time; every player was ready to contribute, no matter how big or small his role would be. Next up was Daniel Boone Little League.

Wednesday, July 20th

It was another 6:00 p.m. game at Moss Wright Park, and the field of eight teams was now down to the final three. Since Columbia had not lost, they were in the driver's seat, awaiting the next game between the winner of Nolensville and Daniel Boone Little League. As the week grew longer, our fans grew stronger. The Daniel Boone game was no exception as another raucous crowd filled the stands. It was no surprise we got off to an early lead in the top of the first with Nash scoring the first run of the game. In the top of the third, our offense exploded with seven unanswered runs. Zeros flooded the box score as Nash's pitching continued to shut down Daniel Boone's offense. Final score: 8-2. Our pitching was dominant as Nash, combined with Caz Logue, gave up zero earned runs. Wright and William led the offensive charge by driving in five out of the eight runs. Another team was eliminated, and what was once a tournament of eight teams was now down to the final two. Three down and two to go! We Believe.

Following our typical post-game huddle down the foul line, the team greeted our families and fans outside the dugout. The stars shining down on a warm summer night were starting to align as this determined team from Nolensville continued to show their resiliency and tenacity. We had one more night in the cabin as a team, and there would be an extra special dinner for us prepared by none other than Chef Randy. As the boys came sprinting into the cabin, there was one thing standing between them and a surprise dinner – shower time! While the team cleaned up, Randy quickly prepared their steak dinners. Each plate was assembled with a bacon-wrapped filet and ear of corn on the cob stacked with butter. Bon Appetit!

Following an amazing dinner, someone had to do the dishes, and it wasn't going to be us coaches. Up stepped the vets of the team to close the door. Typically, Jack and William put their hands to good use on the baseball field, but not this night. As the other boys cleared the table, Jack and William proceeded to hammer out the dishes. We had one more enjoyable night together at the cabin filled with fun, laughter, and even an extended bedtime. With another 6:00 p.m. game the next night and the team checking out of the cabin the next morning, we knew we'd have to keep the boys occupied for the afternoon before we headed for our pre-game activities. There was only one thing on our minds leaving the cabin and that was a rematch with Columbia American Little League. We knew it would be a challenge as their pitchers were well rested, and we had the tough task of beating them twice in a row in order for us to capture another Tennessee State Championship.

Thursday, July 21st

The next morning, the usual wakeup call occurred as the boys had to pack up their bags and clean up the cabin. Unsurprisingly, two nights of a ton of fun also brought loads of trash. While the boys were packing and cleaning up the cabin, the three coaches talked through what was planned for the rest of the day. Mark Carter, Senior Associate Athletic Director at Vanderbilt University, came up with a grand plan. It would be a once in a lifetime experience that the boys would soon encounter.

However, before heading to Vanderbilt University to tour its baseball facility, we headed to Double Dogs for a team lunch. After filling their bellies with some enjoyable food, we took the five-minute drive to the athletic department of Vanderbilt. Mark provided a behind the scenes tour of Vanderbilt baseball's facility which included their pitching lab, classroom, weight room and indoor cages. We also paid a visit to the Vandy Boys players' lounge, coaches' offices, Hawkins Field, and the alumni locker room. Mark provided a thorough play-by-play outlining the details and history of one of college baseball's most storied programs. To sit in the alumni locker room and look at pictures and equipment used by ex-Vandy Boys greats, such as Dansby Swanson, David Price, and Tony Kemp was surreal. For any 11 or 12-year-old baseball player, the dream is to play baseball at Vanderbilt University. For these kids to spend two hours touring the halls of such an elite program was truly a thrilling afternoon to remember.

Following the spectacular tour of the Vanderbilt baseball facility, we made one last stop to get a team picture in front of the giant guitar sign, formerly the scoreboard for the Nashville Sounds minor league baseball team, located near downtown Nashville. However, it was now time to get our game faces on and head back towards Moss Wright Park. A rematch vs. Columbia American Little League was set to begin at 6:00 p.m.

The boys of summer in front of the giant Nashville guitar

The crowd began to shuffle in a few hours before game time as this game was the biggest game of the year for both programs. We knew Columbia American would be rested up and ready to throw their horses as they didn't want to get to an "if" game. As the stands filled up and droves of fans wearing their black and gold sat on the bleachers and lined up down the right field line, so did Columbia's fans, wearing their red attire, on the left. The energy was high, the crowd was boisterous, and these two teams were ready to compete.

It was a must win, and none better than our ace, Jack Rhodes, was set to start this pivotal game. The hit parade continued for the boys from Nolensville as they exploded for three runs in the bottom of the first, thanks to base knocks from Trent McNiel and Josiah Porter. After Columbia stormed back with three unearned runs in the top of the second, the floodgates opened as Nolensville put up seven unanswered runs, highlighted by a towering three-run homer by

Wright Martin. Jack completed the run-ruled shortened game by tossing four innings with 7 K's as Nolensville routed Columbia 14-3. The bats were on fire as Bo, Wright, and William all had multi-hit games and Wright ended up with 4 RBI's. One game, one inning, one AB at a time. Four down and one game to go. After our post-game huddle and warm welcome by parents and fans, there was a definite shift in momentum. We Believe.

Friday, July 22nd

The championship game was here, and Nolensville Little League would be taking on Columbia American Little League for the second night in a row, the third time in the last week. At this point, there were no surprises as we certainly knew all of Columbia's players and who they would most likely pitch that night. Our team was both mentally and physically ready as this would be our biggest game to date. Everything would be left on the diamond as one team would move on to the Southeast Regional in Warner Robins, Georgia, and the other team's LLWS dreams would come to an end. Since it was a Friday night, we expected to see even more of a crowd for the 6:00 p.m. start and, wow, did our crowd ever show up with extra enthusiasm.

Right from the start, the bats responded as Bo crushed a two RBI double to left field that scored two runs. T-Rex followed with another RBI double, and Nolensville was off and running with a 3-0 lead. In the bottom of the first, Columbia American rallied to put up three runs and the score was 3-3 after one inning of play. We knew this was going to be a battle moving forward. We decided to go with T-Rex to start the championship game. He had shown so much poise in prior games and was a go-to pitcher throughout the post season. Trent struggled a bit in the bottom of the first, and after giving up a hit and two walks, Randy decided to pull Trent and replace him with 11-year-old Nash Carter. We could see that Trent, coming off the mound, was disappointed with his performance. However, if there was one player on our team who epitomized what a true team player was, it was T-Rex. As the team came into the dugout following the bottom of the third inning, Trent gathered all the players around him in the dugout. Mark and Randy were standing outside the dugout when they heard a commotion going on. They suddenly turned around and saw Trent talking to the entire team and apologizing for his performance, saying, "Don't let me be the reason we lose this game." Whether T-Rex meant for this to happen or not, I truly believe at that moment his leadership and humbleness put a spark underneath our team and, boy, did they respond. After back-to-back singles by Grayson and William, Drew stepped up and launched another clutch double that scored two more runs. Bo proceeded to drive another runner in; then, Lane followed up with a walk. Up came Josiah with a triple to right field that scored two more runs. At the end of three innings, it was Nolensville 15 and Columbia 3. Although the game was not over, we knew we were only an inning away from run ruling Columbia for the second straight night. One more run came across the top of the fourth inning, and then Nash took the bump in the bottom of the fourth to extend his scoreless inning streak. With two outs and runners on first and second, Jack Rhodes fielded a ground ball at third and stepped on the bag for the final out. Nolensville Little League was once again state champs!

The boys begin to dog pile on one another while the other boys rushed out from the dugout, tossing water into the air. As the dogpile ensued, the scoreboard announcer roared, "Congratulations, Nolensville!" and the three coaches hugged each other with elation. Our fans, who always believed in us, were cheering from the rooftops and patiently waiting to congratulate the team. What many thought would be an impossible feat turned out to be a miraculous comeback filled with teamwork and clutch performances. We Believe.

2022 Tennessee State Little League Baseball Champions

SOUTHEAST REGIONAL – TWO-PEAT

The big state championship win brought much anticipation for what was going to unfold in the upcoming weeks leading up to the Southeast Regional hosted in Warner Robins, Georgia. There would be almost a two-week hiatus between defeating Columbia American to clinch the state championship and playing our first Southeast Regional game on August 4th. Within that period there was a ton of work to be done. There were no breaks in between for the team as we had to prepare the boys for even tougher competition since the regional would bring out the best Little League teams in the Southeast. Little League International and the Southeast Region director and staff would host webinars for the families which included information on what to expect when down in Warner Robins. Information and questionnaires would be gathered on each player and coach so that Little League and ESPN had fun facts to share on their television broadcasts.

Also, there would be intense concentration on fundraising efforts for our team. Coaches and players would have their hotel and meal expenses paid for by Little League International, but we still had to provide our own transportation down to Warner Robins, which was about a 5.5-hour drive. However, families that would be traveling down to Warner Robins had to pay for all their expenses. It was a huge undertaking as parents needed to schedule time off work, coordinate with schools if they were bringing their other kids, and book lodging for their pets. Once down in Warner Robins, families were on their own for lodging, meals, and transportation. Our fundraising efforts would help offset expenses for the 13 families. We knew how supportive our family, friends, and community would be since we conducted fundraising efforts for last year's team. What we didn't predict was how last year's efforts would be outdone by even more generosity and assistance in 2022.

The fundraising efforts began with a bang! From individual player letters sent to family and friends to Nolensville Little League spirit week at various restaurants around town, there would be an influx of people and businesses just looking to give back to the team. Our uniforms and other equipment were donated by such generous individuals and businesses. From sponsorship opportunities for businesses local and afar to a few small-town businesses offering raffle prizes to help generate funding, the outpouring of support was truly overwhelming. One of the biggest fundraising efforts was created and executed by a local business, The Nesting Project and its owner, Corinne Chapman Morse. Last year Corinne created and sold Nolensville Little League All-Star t-shirts, hats, and signs with proceeds going back to the team. This year was no different as her Nolensville Little League All-Star branded items were a home run with the community. There were also donation buckets dropped off at different establishments around town. Every player on the team, not to mention all our incredible team parents, played a role, whether big or small, contributing to the effort. There was an energized buzz around our small town of Nolensville. Little did people know what kind of ride they were about to experience.

When one thinks about our Nolensville Little League baseball family, one can't forget about last year's LLWS team because this was the team that helped put Nolensville on the map. It was a team made up of such incredible young men and families that from the start of the 2022 journey gave so much unconditional support. From parents and players attending district, state, and even regional games to some ex-players throwing live in simulated games helping the team prepare for their next opponent, both players and parents from last year's team were so supportive. What better way, then, to start a new tradition and help with the fundraising efforts than to host an exhibition game between last year's LLWS team and our current squad. When Randy came to Mark and me with the idea, we embraced it and knew it would be a blockbuster of an event.

The first ever Nolensville LLWS alumni game was scheduled for the night of Saturday, July 30th. With very little time to plan, we knew we'd need a lot of help from others to execute this game without a hitch. Earlier that day we received a lot of rain, and, unfortunately, the Nolensville field was not in great condition to play a game. However, we had a back-up plan and were able to use a turf field at another park. The first ever alumni game was not just going to be a tune-up game for our team; rather, it was also meant to be a fundraising event. Craig Dever, father of Lane, and owner of Uncle Bud's Catfish Chicken & Such was going to have his food truck at the Nolensville quad prior to the game. Although the game didn't take place at the Nolensville quad, there was still a huge turnout prior to the game to grab some of the best catfish and chicken in middle Tennessee as the proceeds were going back to the team. Our players and coaches were also there connecting with fans and expressing our gratitude to the families and friends that came out to support the team.

Following a tasty dinner, we took the 15-minute drive out to Cane Ridge. Dressed in our Vandy pin-stripe uniforms, we took the field for warmups. Unfortunately, not all the boys from last year's team were able to make the game, but the majority were there and were styling their 2021 yellow and black LLWS uniforms. It was a reunion for the ages as Coach Chris Mercado came out of retirement to manage the 2021 team. Despite having to move the location a few hours before game time, the crowd grew deep, and the cheering and ovations got louder. After a back-and-forth clash between these two talented teams, the game ended in a 7-7 tie. Regardless of the score, the night of July 30th was a monumental occasion. Having our 2022 team there on the same field as last year's LLWS team brought out inspiration, devotion, and togetherness. Our team looked up to the 2021 team and had so much respect for what they had accomplished the year before. To share the diamond with these super stars would be a moment our players, parents, and coaches would never forget. The alumni game, which will now become a tradition for years to come, was a huge success.

Inaugural Nolensville LLWS alumni game featuring the 2021 and 2022 teams

After capturing the Tennessee State Championship, the town of Nolensville wanted to send off the team by holding a Nolensville Little League State Championship parade throughout town. On Sunday, July 31st , the team and their families met at a local shopping center parking lot and prepared to get escorted by the Nolensville police and fire departments. Fortunately, we had several dads with pickup trucks. Three to four boys per truck jumped into the truck beds, which were decorated in black and gold. Randy and a few boys also drove in his jeep which was rocking our Nolensville star flag. Many of the moms made signs with their kids' names that were proudly displayed on each of the trucks. The parade began and sirens roared down the back streets of Nolensville while our players waved to future Little League all-stars and their families. As the line of trucks made its way down the historic part of downtown Nolensville, I vividly remember seeing the sea of black and gold on both sides of the street with our parents holding fat heads of their sons as well as families, friends, and community members proudly cheering on the team. As the parade route made its way to the ball field parking lot, we were greeted with more applause.

Following the parade, I had all the boys follow me to the front of the dugout on field #2. After speaking to Blake Bivens of the Nolensville Little League, we thought it would be a good idea for the town to get to know each of our Little League All-Stars better. I decided to interview and video all the players and have them introduce themselves, state their position(s), and say their favorite Major League Baseball teams and players. An exercise that I honestly thought would take 15 minutes ended up taking an hour after so many takes and miscues. Nonetheless, despite the longer than anticipated video session, it was really entertaining to see and hear these boys talk on camera. It also, ultimately, prepared them for even more camera time down the road. The videos were eventually posted to the Nolensville Little League Facebook page where fans were able to get to know each of these Little League super stars.

We decided to have one final team dinner at our go to restaurant, Wings to Go, prior to our departure down to Warner Robins, Georgia. That night would be another special night since we had a big revelation in store for the boys. Last year before we headed down, we stunned the kids with a video montage of congratulatory and best wishes from former and current big leaguers, city and town officials, local restaurants and more. After dinner, with help from our coaches, parents, and so many others, all eyes were glued to the flat screen television centered on the wall at Wings to Go. Messages of inspiration and congratulations were proudly delivered by current and former MLB super stars, such as Dansby Swanson, Tony Kemp, and Dave Stewart. Robert Hassell III, South Nashville Little League, 2013-2014 LLWS alum and current Washington Nationals outfielder, provided some motivating words and thoughtful advice. Vanderbilt Athletic Coaches –Tim Corbin, Scott Brown, Clark Lea, and Jerry Stackhouse – also got into the act. Country music stars Sheryl Crow and Thomas Rhett belted out some encouraging verses. Local city officials and high school baseball coaches offered up words of wisdom as well. All in all, a range of over 40 different messages of motivation and well wishes rang through the restaurant as players, parents, and workers watched with beaming smiles. However, this video couldn't have been realized without countless hours of editing and putting it all together from my beloved son, Jack.

Following dinner, the team headed next door to Sweet CeCe's frozen yogurt where the owner of Sweet CeCe's and Corinne from the Nesting Project put together a raffle to help support the fundraising efforts. The boys were chosen as the lucky ones to pick each winner as so many local restaurants and establishments provided gift cards for prizes. It was a fun-filled night for sure, but we also knew an early morning was upon us as the next day we were heading south to Warner Robins to take care of some business.

Bright and early the next morning the team and their families met in the parking lot of Nolensville High School. We had a 5.5-hour drive ahead of us and little did the boys know how they would be getting to their final destination. With the help of Mark Carter, the team would be traveling down to Georgia in style – Vandy Boys style. Our team bus down south would be none other than the Vanderbilt Athletics bus. Wrapped with the Vanderbilt logos across both sides, this bus was top notch both inside and out. The boys were extremely excited to say the least as this bus ride would be another special bonding experience for these 13 kids and us coaches. Bags were loaded, coolers were stocked, and the boys said their final farewells to their families. Dressed in their Nolensville Little League star hats and shirts, they headed up the bus steps, enthusiastically calling out dibs on their seats. As the bus door closed, our Nolensville Little League All-Star families cheered and waved emphatically as our bus headed out.

During the 5.5-hour ride down south all the boys kept occupied. The coaches sat towards the front of the bus, and, undoubtedly, there was a ton of laughter and entertainment coming from the back. Always thinking ahead, the coaches wanted to ensure the boys were somewhat prepared with questions they may be asked by the media going into the Southeast Regional. One by one, we had each player come sit by the coaches as I pretended to be a local sports reporter and peppered them with a few questions. "What makes this team so special?" and "How's the experience been so far?" were the two questions I asked each player. The words that came out of their mouths were pure and passionate. For some, thoughts came so naturally, and for others many takes were recorded. However, there were so many commonalities amongst their responses. What made this team so unique was not just the talent displayed on the diamond, but also, more importantly, was the strong bond built with each other. Every player looked after each other and picked each other up no matter the situation. When I was thumbing through these priceless videos on my phone, there was one that stood out more than any other. First baseman, Wright Martin, summed it up so eloquently when he said, "This team is so special because we have a lot of energy in the dugout and love for each other. If one guy doesn't get the job done, the second guy will; the third guy will. It's kind of like an energy train that we have in our dugout. Secondly, this experience has been once in a lifetime. It's been a great time hanging out with my friends in the hotel, and just enjoying it." Words like love, friends, energy and once in a lifetime that Wright conveyed really embodied what this team was all about as well as the journey we encountered throughout the summer.

As the Vanderbilt bus pulled up to the Hampton Inn in Warner Robins, all eyes were on Nolensville Little League. For William, Jack, Randy, and me, it was a year ago when we stepped foot into the same hotel as one of eight teams representing the Southeast. However, fortunately, for this year's team, the dreaded COVID-19 testing station was not awaiting them. Right off the bat, we could tell the experience was going to be much different as testing for COVID-19 every other day and mandatory masks were no longer required. However, we still proceeded with caution and tried to separate our team and their families as much as possible, especially indoors. During the bus ride, we provided the boys with their rooming assignments and expectations while staying at the hotel. We knew there would be a lot of other teams and parents staying there. Knowing that we were not just representing our team, but also our families, Nolensville Little League, our community, and the entire state of Tennessee, our expectations for our team's behavior were extremely high.

The team riding in style to Warner Robins, Georgia, and the Southeast Regional

As the boys headed up to their rooms, the three coaches also checked into their individual rooms. As I unpacked my bags and laid out some of the remaining food and drinks from the bus ride, I thought back to how much fun the team had last year while playing and, eventually, winning the Southeast Regional. I was extremely excited for this team and what they were about to encounter. Now that we had arrived and our families were close behind, we knew the competition was going to be steep, and there was going to be a target on our backs once again since we were the defending Southeast Regional Champions. State champs from Florida, Georgia, Alabama, South Carolina, North Carolina, Virginia, and West Virginia were all at the hotel and ready for the week ahead. Following dinner that night, we gave the boys some time to hang out, get acquainted with their new rooms and roommates, and, ultimately, have some fun. Mark and I oversaw getting the boys ready for bed and making sure they complied with our rules. Like last year, before bedtime each night, we had the boys write in their daily journals. For most of the boys, when their pen or pencil hit the paper, their words and thoughts came out with ease. For a few, it was like pulling teeth to get them to focus, let alone write legibly in their journals, but all in all, the journal-writing experience turned out to be a collection of some of their most memorable moments and something they will look back at in years to come. Finally, a good night's sleep was needed with most of the day spent traveling and a full day of activities ahead the next day.

The dining accommodations provided at the Southeast Regional in Warner Robins were remarkable. Lunches throughout the week were provided by Little League and catered in at the Southeast headquarters cafeteria. I remember the first time stepping into Little League's headquarters where we ate lunch and noticed a framed picture of all of last year's teams on the front lobby wall. Centered in the middle of the other seven state champions was a picture of the 2021 Nolensville Little League team holding their Southeast Regional Champion banner. Once this picture was noticed, all our boys gravitated to this wall to take a glimpse. Each and every kid on our team was thinking the same thing that all three coaches were believing. This time next year, there would be another Nolensville team pictured so proudly on the walls of the Southeast headquarters.

It was always a pleasure lining up for lunch and speaking with the various volunteers giving their valued time to feed the participating teams. Georgia Ritchie, a long-tenured volunteer at the Southeast Little League Park, was adored. Always so accommodating to the kids and coaches, Georgia became a favorite for our Nolensville team and families. Georgia was also known for her pins as she had been collecting various Little League pins for years. Last year, due to the pandemic, we were unable to pin trade at the Southeast Regional. However, 2022 was a different story, and Randy had designed two different pins. It was awesome to participate in another Little League tradition as we exchanged pins with the other teams at the Southeast Regional and were even able to add to Georgia's pin collection.

This year was a bit different from last year when it came to dinner, though. Little League provided each team with gift cards, so we were on our own when it came to providing dinner for the team. It was the typical eleven-and-twelve-year-old types of food throughout the week – Dominoes, Chipotle, Chick-fil-A (multiple times) and subs. The boys had it made since there were also various snacks and drinks in their rooms for late night munching.

As the wake-up calls took place, room by room, players started scurrying down the stairwell to get in line at the hotel's breakfast buffet. The schedule for today was practice and a visit to the Southeast Regional headquarters and Little League Southeast Park. All our practices took place at a local ballpark located in front of the Southeast Regional's complex. We also took a tour of the stadium and captured many team pictures along the way. In addition, we had the pleasure of introducing the boys to one of the longstanding ushers whom we got to know last year. Gary Kay, better known as Papa Smurf, has been a Little League volunteer for over 27 years. Not only did he volunteer as an usher during the Southeast Regional, but also, he served as an usher and Little League ambassador in Williamsport at the Little League World Series. Remembered for his noticeable white beard and love for the game, our players, coaches, and parents all hit it off with Papa Smurf throughout the summer of 2022. One of Papa Smurf's famous quotes regarding the Little League World Series was, "Until you partake in it, you don't understand." So true his words were.

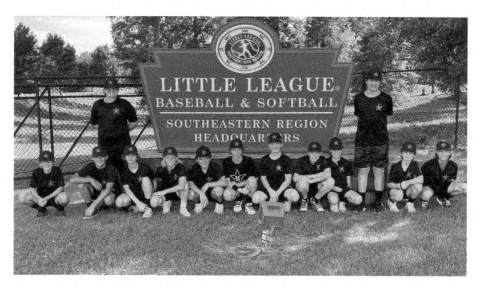

Team picture in front of the Little League Southeastern Region Headquarters sign

For most of these boys the Little League Southeast Park, a venue actually used only for the Southeast Regional games for Little League baseball and softball, would be the biggest venue and most exquisite field they had ever stepped foot on. The field itself was in immaculate condition and was maintained like a major league diamond, in which the grounds crew held great pride. It even had a smaller hill in the outfield where kids could slide down on cardboard similar to scenes often seen in Williamsport.

Opening-day ceremonies began with a few local dignitaries speaking and each of the eight teams being introduced. One of the most exciting moments of the ceremony was when all eyes looked up in the sky as an F-15 Eagle from Robins Airforce Base did a fly over. Once the ceremonies ended, the day grew longer in anticipation of the first-round games of the Southeast Regional.

Throughout the week, dinner was always served in the hotel's conference room on the first floor. After dinner that night, the boys headed back to their rooms while the three coaches met in Randy's room and talked about our game plan for Alabama. We were hours away from our opening game vs. Alabama and knew we couldn't take the team from Sylacauga Little League lightly despite beating them 23-0 in the opening round last year. The night was coming to an end, and Mark and I made sure the boys logged their day in their journals, settled down, and got a good night's sleep.

Thursday, August 4th

Finally, it was game day! I recall waking up and seeing all our hotel room doors plastered in black and gold. Posters were decorated with the boys' names, motivational thoughts, and words of encouragement. There was a common word on every room's poster...Believe. It was an awesome gesture from Maren Rhodes, mother of Jack, and was appreciated by the entire team.

Unfortunately, the Vanderbilt Athletics bus had to head back to Nashville, but we were fortunate to use a sprinter van (owned by two of our parents – Jason McNiel and Craig Dever) and the Nissan Armada, which was generously donated by a local car dealership, as our means of transportation for the rest of the week. Before departing for the ballpark, a new tradition was introduced to the boys. During last year's LLWS run, each player and coach took a swig of a special mouthwash. The routine started in Warner Robins during the Southeast Regional and continued throughout the LLWS. For everyone but us, it was a standard run-of-the-mill mouthwash that gave one fresh breath. Before each game I went around with little paper cups filled with TheraBreath's Clean Mint mouthwash for the players to swish. Call it superstition or wanting our kids to have fresh breath since we weren't exactly sure if they had brushed their teeth the night before, this superstition stuck for the rest of our journey. Once our mouths were fresh, we caravanned to the field while blasting our go to pump-up song: "Get Buck in Here" by DJ Felli Fel. As the kids were getting revved up while singing and dancing along, there was one thing on our minds: Alabama.

Our team was ready; parents and families were filled with excitement and our community back home was ready to watch feverishly on national television as all regional games were being shown on ESPN+. All these boys (except for William and Jack) had never played on television, let alone a nationally televised game on ESPN+.

We decided to go with one of our veterans to start the first game of the tournament: William Satinoff. Based on his experience, poise, and ability to throw strikes, we thought William would be best suited for the opener. After a scoreless first inning, Nolensville exploded for three runs in the top of the second, thanks to some sloppy defense by Alabama. Sati threw the first two innings giving up no hits and no runs. After consecutive multi-run innings led by Lane Dever's two RBI double, Josiah Porter closed the door by coming in relief of William and throwing three scoreless innings, giving up no hits and striking out all nine batters. This was the first time we used Josiah on the mound during our post season, and, man, did he come through and throw a gem. It was a no hitter for Sati and Jo-Jo as Nolensville brought the lumber and scored eleven runs en route to a game-shortened 11-0 victory over Alabama. Nash, Bo, Lane, and Drew each had two hits while Lane and Drew also drove in two runs. What a way to start off the Southeast Regional tournament.

Earlier that day South Carolina defeated Florida 2-1. Friday would bring a powerhouse matchup between us and South Carolina. Northwood Little League won the South Carolina state championship last year and was back in Warner Robins for a second year in a row. Nolensville and Northwood were the only two teams to make it back to the Southeast Regional from last year. We Believe.

Friday, August 5th

In any other year these 13 boys from Nolensville Little League would be attending their first day of school. Not this year, though, as a showdown between Tennessee and South Carolina was on the docket with a 4:00 p.m. EST game time. In customary fashion, when the team arrived at the ballpark, we had each of them take a picture with the stadium in the background holding a sign that read "first day of school."

After scouting South Carolina days prior, we knew they were deep in pitching and were a very well-coached squad. We also knew that during their scrappy win vs. Florida, they had used up three of their top pitchers. However, because of their depth, we couldn't take anything for granted and knew this would be a really tough matchup for us. Right from the start, we knew this was going to be a back-and-forth affair. Trent McNiel took the bump for us and pitched his heart out. After five consecutive innings of no run ball, we were tied 0-0 heading into the sixth inning. It was a pitcher's duel to remember as both teams' offenses were stymied. The top of the sixth inning began with a base hit to left field by Jack Rhodes. Drew Chadwick followed with a scorcher to left field as Rhodes advanced to third and was called out. Clearly, Jack's foot got under the tag, and after the play was reviewed, the call was overturned. Pinch hitter JF Forni came to the plate and was intentionally walked. With bases loaded and no outs, we had South Carolina on the ropes. Our dugout, which was fairly quiet for the entire game, all of a sudden came alive with energy as "We Believed." Our fans rose to their feet and the stadium got louder and louder as Trent came to the plate. With the infield in, T-Rex hit a 1-1 curveball and belted it to centerfield scoring two runs. As the throw got past the catcher, JF hustled home to make it a 3-0 lead. It was so great to see Trent, who pitched the game of his life, help himself out with such a clutch, game-winning hit. Jack Rhodes, who came in relief of T-Rex in the fifth inning, pitched a 1-2-3 bottom of the sixth inning to close the door for a tremendous hard-fought victory.

The South Carolina boys and coaches were first class despite a tough defeat. Staying on the same floor at the Hampton Inn, our boys got to know some of their team. I also became friendly with their coaches during the week, and our friendship grew throughout the summer.

We were now 2-0 in the double elimination tournament, and with a day off on Saturday, we were able to get some practice in, watch two elimination games, and get some well-needed rest. Our next game would be another huge test as Harris County Little League out of Georgia was also 2-0. Sunday couldn't get here soon enough as all eyes would be on this powerhouse matchup. We Believe.

Saturday, August 6th

There was a ton of anticipation for the two games being played at the Little League Southeast Park today. The first game was an elimination game wherein Virginia squeezed out a 6-4 win over a very talented North Carolina squad. The loser of the game between us and Georgia would play Virginia on Monday in another elimination game. Winner of the Tennessee vs. Georgia game would automatically head to the Southeast Regional championship game slated for Tuesday, August 9th, live on ESPN. As for previous games, the coaches met the night before to review prior game film as well as strategize for this very talented Georgia squad. Only 1.5 hours away from Warner Robins, we knew the Harris County team would have a lot of fans present and bring a boisterous crowd. Our fans were equally ready to bring the noise and show massive support for the boys from Nolensville. The community was also set as Mill Creek Brewery was holding one of their many watch parties throughout the LLWS run.

After a lengthy rain delay, our ace on the staff and savvy veteran, Jack Rhodes, towed the rubber in the top of the first inning. The first pitch of the game resulted in a lead-off double by Georgia, followed by an RBI triple, giving Georgia a 1-0 lead to start the game. In the bottom of the first, three consecutive batters got on by walk or hit-by-pitch leading to a bases loaded situation with Bo Daniel stepping to the plate. On a 1-1 count, Bo-Bo launched a fastball and clobbered an opposite field grand slam giving Nolensville a 4-1 lead. As the boys sprinted out to home plate to greet Bo as he crossed home plate, we suddenly felt the momentum shift; our crowd was standing in jubilation, waving their "We Believe" signs and screaming feverishly.

Decorated "We Believe" signs were always present during our LLWS run

After the bases were loaded in the top of the second inning with one out, Randy headed to the mound to give, quite possibly, one of the greatest pep talks in Little League history. Randy passionately enunciated, "Smell the roses and blow out the candles." This heart-to-heart chat was meant to calm Jack down, reinforce that he was in control and encourage him to throw some strikes. Little did Randy know his "smell the roses and blow out the candles" exchange would go viral on social media and cause such a frenzy. After another base-on-balls and run scored, Randy made his second straight visit to the mound to relieve Jack and bring in none other than Nash Carter. Nash had been one of our most consistent pitchers to date, and the three coaches had the utmost confidence in a pressure-packed situation for him to get the job done. With arguably the best hitter in Georgia's lineup coming to the plate with the bases loaded, a super composed Nash threw a slow breaking ball which resulted in a 6-4 ground ball force out to close the inning.

When one talks about clutch performances throughout the LLWS journey, this one certainly rises to the top.

As the game went on, so did our bats as Nolensville exploded for nine runs and, ultimately, defeated Georgia by the score of 9-3. The offense was led by Bo Daniel who had two hits, including a grand slam and five total RBI's. Wright Martin also went deep as he launched a mammoth bomb to right center field that hit off the light post in the bottom of the fifth inning. Nash Carter came in relief of Jack & Cheese and absolutely dominated. He threw 4.1 innings and only gave up 1 run. The "W" over Georgia was a perfect example of players picking each other up and battling through adversity. We were now heading to the Southeast Regional Championship for the second year in a row. We Believe.

The next day was an off day for the team. From the start, we had a busy schedule and wanted to head to the stadium and watch Georgia take on Virginia since the winner would take us on for the championship. Every time we made it back to the stadium as spectators we watched in unity, or the boys would collectively head to the outfield grass to watch the game. Like many other games that week, the Georgia vs. Virginia game was another exciting one. Virginia ended up winning 4-1 and would take on Nolensville on Tuesday, August 9th at 5:00 p.m. EST live on ESPN. Back home the excitement was also brewing as local news stations interviewed Randy and some of the players in anticipation of the championship game. Following lunch at the Southeast Regional's cafeteria, we decided to have some team bonding outside the ballpark and hotel. *Top Gun: Maverick* was playing at a local theater and despite it being seen by most of the boys already, we thought it would still be a great time to connect. Later that night, we had one more dinner together as a team and knew it would be a fairly early night for the boys with the championship game looming.

Tuesday, August 9th

The day had arrived, and there was a ton of excitement in the air. After eating breakfast and taking it easy for most of the day, we headed to the field in our caravan. As both team vehicles pulled out of the Hampton Inn parking lot, we were greeted with cheers and applause from our team's parents and families.

When we made it to the complex, like every other pre-game, we went directly to the outdoor cages where Mark and I threw BP. There would be more television coverage since it was the championship game. ESPN cameras spanned up and down as our players took their final swings in the cage. Walking over to the stadium from the cages, the team was extremely focused. We knew it would be a dog fight since Virginia was throwing its ace.

After a 1-2-3 top of the first inning for Nolensville, Jack Rhodes took the bump in the bottom of the first inning. We decided to go back to Jack since he didn't go over his pitch count in the Georgia game. We were also confident that he was going to come back with a vengeance. However, after Jack's first pitch, Randy noticed him wince a bit. Following a lead-off walk, Randy called timeout, and headed to the mound. Earlier in the week Jack was hit by a pitch in the right shoulder and was battling some stiffness and discomfort throughout the week. As Randy got to the hill, Jack was visibly upset. Being the fierce competitor Jack is, we knew he wanted to continue and not let his team down, but it was definitely the right move to take him out as he was grimacing in distress. Ultimately, we decided to call on Drew Chadwick to pitch in the biggest game of his young career. Drew had given us some strong, clutch outings throughout the post season. He showed a lot of poise and displayed grit during our district run vs. Goodlettsville and was an intense competitor. As Randy handed Drew the baseball, he calmly said, "Hey, we believe in you." Believe we did as Drew ended up pitching one of the greatest games of his life. Back and forth, the next three innings brought goose eggs for each team. Virginia's ace was in a zone, striking out our hitters with swings and misses. After giving up the two runs in the first inning, Drew settled down and was in control throwing strikes and mowing down the Virginia batters.

Into the top of the fifth we went, down 2-0. With one out, up stepped Josiah Porter. Jo-Jo belted a line drive down the left field line for a stand-up double. Until then our boys looked puzzled as Virginia's ace was pitching an absolute gem. On a 3-2 count, Wright Martin hammered a line drive to left field scoring Josiah for our first run of the game. These were big back-to-back, clutch base knocks from Josiah and Wright against, arguably, the best pitcher in the tournament. Our crowd, which had been silent for most of the game, came to life as the lead was cut to one and the Virginia ace's pitch count was nearing the end. After a beautiful 1-6-3 double play and another Chadwick strikeout in the bottom of the 5th inning, we had one more chance to put some runs on the board.

Before the top of the 6th inning began, Randy gathered the team and said, "We are a locomotive, and we are going full speed. Let's write our own story and put a bunch of runs on the board and win a region championship right now." As William and Jack shouted, "We What?", the team proudly responded by saying, "We Believe!" We had our 2-3-4 hitters in the lineup coming up. As I stepped in the third base coaching box, I looked over and saw William adjusting his batting gloves. I had all the confidence in the world he was going to get on base and start this rally. With a 1-1 count, Sati delivered with a ground ball base hit down the third base line. Jack & Cheese followed with a scorcher down the right field line which sent William sliding into third base. As the throw went over the third baseman's head, William hustled home and slid in with the game-tying run. Pounding his chest, waving his arms to the ardent crowd, and pointing at Jack on third base acknowledging that he was the man, William was greeted by his enthusiastic teammates. Jack ended up on third with his fist clenched in the air with jubilation as the two veterans came through once again with clutch performances. As chants of "Black – Gold" erupted from our crowd, the floodgates were about to open. After a well-deserved intentional walk to Bo Daniel, Caz Logue ripped a hot-shot single to the shortstop, which scored the game winning run. Two more runs scored on a wild pitch and Wright Martin's RBI single, and we were headed into the bottom of the sixth inning with a 5-2 lead over Virginia. Chadwick took the bump in the bottom of the sixth inning and gave up a base hit to lead off the inning. After a ground out to first base, Virginia had a man on second base with one out. The next Virginia batter battled Drew back and forth, fouling off consecutive pitches. On a 2-2 count and his 84 and final pitch of the game, a line drive was hit to right field as Logue tracked it down. Caz immediately threw to second base as the runner took off at the crack of the bat expecting the ball to drop. The throw cruised over second base and into the glove of Chadwick who was backing up. Drew suddenly tossed the ball to William who emphatically stomped his left foot on the bag for the double play and final out of the game.

Chaos ensued as the boys from Tennessee threw their gloves in the air and started the dog pile in front of the pitcher's mound. When the last play concluded, I jumped up with such excitement that I hit my head on the dugout light fixture. Luckily, I have a hard head and had so much adrenaline pumping through my veins that I really didn't feel much pain until later that night. The three coaches embraced each other. Nolensville Little League had just punched their ticket to Williamsport for the second straight year in a row! We Believe.

Celebrating after defeating Virginia, 5-2, to capture the 2022 Southeast Championship

Following the game, the customary lineup of both teams for handshakes began as great sportsmanship was always the standard in Little League play. Once we shook the hands of Virginia, all the players and coaches headed to the backstop screen to greet our families. A brief ceremony took place where the Little League Southeast director presented the team with the Southeast Little League Champion banner and the Southeast Little League World Series jersey. We then trotted out to the left field grass to have our traditional post-game huddle. With all the boys on one knee, the Southeast Championship banner draped across Josiah's shoulders, and Jack Rhodes proudly holding the Nolensville star flag, Randy began his post-game address, and Mark and I followed with some words of our own. Proud was an understatement on how we felt about this team and what they had just achieved.

As we walked off the pristine outfield grass, we were welcomed by our families and fans. For the duration of the regional, we tried to limit a lot of contact with family members as a precaution to keep the boys from getting sick. However, this special moment called for an exception as these 13 boys embraced moms, dads, siblings, grandparents, and friends with hugs and high fives. I'll always remember the smiles of elation plastered on our parents' faces. It not only was our team's win, but also a win and Southeast title shared with these dedicated parents and families, a Nolensville community back home that proudly supported us from day one, the middle Tennessee area, the great state of Tennessee, and now the entire Southeast region.

Following the game, one of the ushers, Pinkie, approached many of the moms and handed them a $100 donation for our upcoming trip to Williamsport. It was so rewarding to hear him and other ushers speak so highly of our boys. Next, a team dinner was in store, and all our players and their families met at a local restaurant for a celebratory dinner. During our dinner, I recall looking up at one of the television screens that was tuned to ESPN, and seeing Nolensville, Tennessee, broadcast as the first team to punch its ticket heading to the Little League World Series. What a memorable sight to see, and it was surely a night to remember. Dreams really do come true.

One of my fondest memories from the regional was the relationships we made with Northwood Little League's players and coaches. Once they were eliminated, South Carolina became some of Nolensville Little League's biggest fans.

They followed our game vs. Georgia on their bus ride home as I received congratulatory texts from their coaches once we won. Some of our players corresponded with theirs, and they also received texts wishing them good luck vs. Virginia. Back home in Taylors (right outside Greenville, SC) the Northwood Little League All-Star team and their families held a watch party for us when we played in the championship game vs. Virginia. When the final out was recorded, their players were ecstatic. To this day, I still go back and watch that video sent to me by their head coach. Throughout our run at the Little League World Series, I continued to receive texts of well wishes and congratulations from their coaches. Their camaraderie and support portrayed a true example of great sportsmanship and how sports can lead to special friendships.

We had no time to spare the morning after our championship win as we were ready to head back home. Following the big win and celebration the night before, the Little League Southeast director and his staff met with our parents in their conference room. The intent of the meeting was to discuss what's next for the team in terms of logistics, things to bring to Williamsport, and timing. Unlike last year when we traveled straight from Georgia to South Williamsport, Pennsylvania, we drove our caravan of boys and coaches back up I-75 and met our parents at the Nolensville Recreation Center later that afternoon. The drive back home included many interviews with local and national media outlets. It would be just the start as Randy and the team probably took part in over a hundred radio, television, and newspaper interviews during the course of the LLWS. We had very little time to recover from a long week in Warner Robins as Little League International was sending a bus from Williamsport the next morning to pick up our team. Families got home that evening, unpacked their sons' bags, and started many loads of laundry as preparation began for a long stay ahead in Williamsport. This year was going to be even more special than ever as it was the 75th anniversary of the Little League World Series.

2022 Southeast Little League Baseball Champions

NOLENSVILLE MEETS WILLIAMSPORT

The next morning the team and their parents headed to the Cool Springs mall parking lot where the Little League International bus was going to pick us up. We had a 12-plus hour bus ride ahead of us, so we were certainly prepared with coolers of drinks and plenty of snacks. After parents and family members joyfully squeezed their kids with one last hug, we were en route to the baseball mecca – described as Disneyworld for young and old baseball fans – Williamsport, Pennsylvania, and the Little League World Series headquarters. The drive to Williamsport was uneventful. The boys stayed occupied on their devices, some took naps, and others just chatted up a storm. Of course, we had stops for meals, and, fortunately, there was a clean bathroom onboard the bus.

While we were traveling hundreds of miles on a bus to Williamsport, our Little League parents were also feverishly planning to get up to Williamsport. Anticipating the best, families had to coordinate travel, hotel accommodations, pet lodging, and vacation off work for up to three potential weeks. It was a hectic, but quite exciting time for our Nolensville parents and their families.

Our bus ride continued throughout the night while more rest and relaxation occurred. As Williamsport grew closer, and we were just minutes from pulling up to the Little League International's campus, the boys were super excited and anxious to step foot off the bus. As we made our last stop in front of the security gates leading into the dormitories, a Little League official walked up the bus staircase, welcomed the team, and informed us that we all had to get a health screening before we departed the vehicle. From what we were told previously, there was going to be no COVID-19 testing throughout the LLWS, so it was a bit of shock when one of Little League's medical officials boarded the bus and started taking our temperatures.

Following all the temp checks, each player and coach impatiently scooted off the bus as all our bags began getting loaded onto carts. Before we could enter the sacred grounds, we still had to go through a metal detector, one by one. Little League International's living quarters for all 20 teams are better known as The International Grove. There was 24/7 security and every player and coach had to go through a metal detector and screening process every time they entered the facility.

It was now 10:45 p.m. EST, and despite a long bus ride across the country, our boys were full of energy and curiosity. We were escorted to our dormitory where we were eagerly greeted by Team Mexico. Even though there was a clear language barrier, the smiles, fist bumps, and attempts to speak some Spanish by some of our players made for such a memorable first impression at the 2022 Little League World Series. We enjoyed hanging out and eating some late-night pizza with our suitemates until we had to call it a night. Before the lights went out and the boys settled into their new beds, we were greeted and welcomed by one of Little League International's directors. He was also accompanied by Uncle Marlin, one of our team hosts that we'd have for the duration of our LLWS stay. Little did we know that night the impact and relationship our players and coaches would have with both Uncle Marlin and our other team host, Uncle Chuck.

We were one of the first teams to arrive at Williamsport. The living quarters consisted of numerous quad-styled dormitories. The front of each dorm had a placard indicating where each team was from. The dorm directly above our Southeast dorm housed the Little League champions from the Caribbean, Curacao. Adjacent to the Curacao dorms were the champions out of the Midwest, Iowa. Lastly, across from our dorms on the bottom floor was the team from Mexico.

Inside each dormitory were two coaches' rooms with individual bathrooms and televisions. Mark and I shared a room throughout the stay in Williamsport. Fortunately, we got along so well and withstood each other's antics. Randy flew solo like the arrangements I had last year. Down the hall from the two coaches' rooms was the larger room where all the boys slept. Originally set up across each wall were multiple bunkbeds where the kids called dibs as soon as they stepped foot into the room. However, after an unfortunate accident with another team days into our stay, all the beds became single beds and were lined up across the room. The bathroom, which had multiple stalls, sinks, and showers, was shared between our team and Team Mexico.

There were stringent rules with which all teams had to comply. No eating or drinking was allowed in the dorms unless it was bottled water. Like at home, the boys needed to keep their areas clean and clothes off the floor. Taking pictures, videos, and facetiming was prohibited inside the dorms. Well, let's just say all the rules were broken probably within the first few days except the ones about taking pictures and videos. Constant clothes on the floor, wet bathing suits hanging from the corners of bunk beds, used towels bundled up in the corner, opened Gatorade bottles and chip wrappers, and much more became the norm around the dorm. Despite having a big yellow garbage bin for dirty clothes in the middle of the room, the boys often decided to put their dirty clothes in other spots. During our dorm life, I would often wonder what these kids' rooms looked at home.

The dorms were a place to not only sleep, but also for the kids to "chill," a word that I got so familiar with during our stay in Williamsport. The boys continued to jot down some of their favorite memories from the day in their journals. Mark and I would do a bedtime check 20 minutes before the lights went out and always read over the boys' journal entries. Reading their journals not only became routine, but also provided much comedy for us coaches. We had a much better understanding of the lingo used by the boys, such as "chilled," "bus," and "mid," coming out of the World Series.

In the center of the campus was the cafeteria and during our stay at the International Grove we started to get a feel for what MLB players ate when they got fed in the clubhouse. Well, maybe not to the level of major leaguers, however, we did get taken care of with a wide selection of breakfast, lunch, and dinner choices. Never once was there just one dish, but rather an assortment, and always the go-to sandwich of peanut butter and jelly. Some of our boys' favorites were pancakes, mac & cheese (Jack Rhodes often had 2-3 servings), tacos, spaghetti, and sloppy joe sandwiches. Dessert was always a must as there were a few coolers filled with assorted ice cream bars, and the coaches' favorite, the famous Nutty Buddy bars. Unfortunately for us three, the dining hall ran out of our go-to ice cream bar a few too many times. The Pennsylvania College of Technology staff always tried to offer healthy options as well. There were always salads, and the drink selections were plentiful with Gatorade, juice, water, and milk (including chocolate). Suffice it to say, Pennsylvania College of Technology students had their hands full as they worked to fill the stomachs of the 20 teams and team hosts.

One of the top moments in the dining hall was the interaction we had with workers and the other teams that were dining. Whether it was the cooks behind the counter serving us, dining room staff, or the team hosts, there were always copious conversations. Specific dining hall rules were instituted from years past, and other teams implemented their own routines. For instance, no hats on heads were ever allowed in the dining hall. Often teams came with no hats, or in some cases, teams left their hats on the window ledge in the area leading into the dining hall. For the Southeast, we came with our own set of rules straight from the Volunteer State. For instance, after each meal, we assigned one or two boys to clean up our tables. Chairs always had to be pushed in, and on some occasions, the coaches got extra help with the boys taking up their trays.

However, the dining hall wasn't just a place to eat, mingle, and enjoy each other's company; it was a bit of a Little League shrine. On the back wall, framed pictures of each LLWS champion, dating from 1947 through the most recent Taylor, Michigan championship in 2021, were proudly hung. Often, I would see players from across the globe walking up and down, staring at the championship pictures, optimistically dreaming that their team's picture would be hanging there some day.

There were also many things to do on the campus to keep the three hundred plus Little Leaguers, managers, coaches, and translators busy. Amongst the attractions were a refreshing junior Olympic size pool and a recreation room with various video games and ping pong tables. There was also an outdoor area called the bullpen located behind the health clinic. Teams would often use these grounds as a wiffle ball field, spending countless hours competing against one another. There were other fun activities set up in the bullpen for the kids to enjoy, but wiffle ball was everyone's favorite. Lastly, there was a laundry facility and health center where there was a medical professional present 24/7. Outside the gates of the Grove stood the iconic Howard J. Lamade Stadium. Adjacent to Lamade was the second stadium on campus: Volunteer Stadium. On top of the famed hill where kids are known to slide down was Little League International headquarters with its museum located across the parking lot. It's definitely a true statement when LLWS participants, following their experience in Williamsport, say it is like being a kid at Disneyworld.

The team played many fun wiffle ball games at the Bullpen

THE UNSUNG SUPERSTARS – THE LLWS TEAM HOSTS

Every morning we were welcomed by our two fantastic team hosts, Uncle Marlin and Uncle Chuck. Team hosts, better known as a team "uncle" or "aunt" have been part of the LLWS for the past 70 years. In 2021, instead of being assigned to a particular team, the uncles were assigned to various duties. Luckily for me, I had the distinct pleasure of meeting Uncle Marlin that year and sharing baseball Hall of Fame stories with him as we both shared a passion for the historic museum. We exchanged a few text messages following last year's world series. Little did we know our paths would cross again a year later.

The day for team hosts typically began early in the morning around 7:00 a.m. and sometimes did not end until 11:00 p.m., depending on whether their team played in a night game. The team hosts were responsible for ensuring that each team was on time for games and practices. They assisted with the coordination of various media activities, helped with laundry, and, ultimately, made sure that many other day-to-day tasks went smoothly for the players, coaches, and managers. Always escorting the teams around the Little League World Series complex, team hosts were some of the LLWS participant's biggest advocates. What makes team hosts even more special and unique is that all their time and dedication is done on a volunteer basis. Without these supportive and caring team hosts, the Little League World Series would not be a thing.

Back in June 2022, when preparation began for the Little League World Series, the team hosts met at Little League International's headquarters to determine which team would be assigned to them come August. Twenty team hosts drew baseballs with a corresponding region's or country's name written on them from a bucket. Fortunately for us, Uncle Marlin picked the right baseball as the Southeast was pulled from the bottom of the bucket. In addition to all the standard responsibilities that came with being a team host, we were very lucky because Uncle Marlin and Uncle Chuck went way above the call of duty for our boys and coaches from Nolensville. There was a relationship like no other, right from the start. Our players and coaches gravitated to these two fine gentlemen like green on grass. From Uncle Marlin taking Randy to get fitted for a tuxedo during an off day to Uncle Chuck taking the boys on his notorious walkabouts around the hallowed Little League grounds, the friendships created with both these uncles will be forever treasured.

Uncle Marlin Cromley, Air Force veteran, retired executive who worked in the athletic and alumni development for Bloomsburg University and Pennsylvania College of Technology, and all-around baseball enthusiast, has been part of the Little League World Series for the past 21 years. Years ago, the president of Little League baseball, Steve Kenner, approached him at an MLB Player's Alumni Association golf tournament where Marlin volunteered. During their conversation, the Little League president discussed the duties and responsibilities of a team host and suggested that Marlin place his name on the waiting list. Nearly 10 years later in 1999 he received a phone call from Little League International asking if he was still interested in volunteering as a team host. Uncle Marlin discussed the opportunity with his wife, Brenda, and she firmly said, "If you don't do this, you will regret it for the rest of your life." If Uncle Marlin had to sum up in one word what it means to be a team host, he says it would be "friendships." He takes pride and considers it to be a privilege that Little League International entrusts him to be an ambassador to represent its organization. The friendships along the way with fellow uncles and aunts, ushers, security, kitchen staff, housekeeping, and grounds crew, along with the lasting friendships of managers, coaches, and players has meant the world to Uncle Marlin. The past 21 years of being an uncle has allowed him to play a small role in the experience of teams coming to Williamsport. These lasting friendships have translated into invitations to attend college graduations and weddings, receive birth announcements, and have the good fortune to just stay in touch with so many national and international team members, families, coaches, and managers. Asked to describe the Little League World Series, Marlin replied, "There is no substitute for such a unique experience. It's a very, very special event and one that has given my wife and me many friends throughout the world."

Uncle Chuck DeLuca has been involved with coaching youth programs within his own community of Clemmons, North Carolina, for the past 30 years. Uncle Chuck claims it wasn't until he started utilizing those principles that are taught, through this game, into his own personal and business life that everything started to change, positively, for him. His success allowed him to be part of the ultimate father-son experience as a 2002 Little League World Series coach while continuing to locally serve his community in the best way he knows how. In the summer of 2005, a simple question posed to a teammate's brother inspired his life into a direction he never dreamed possible. The answer not only left him speechless but called him into action to locally start an adaptive baseball program for athletes with physical and intellectual challenges, serving as their coach – a role in which he continues to date. His role with Little League was broadened in 2005 by an invitation to bring his Challenger League to play in the World Series Exhibition Game on Championship Saturday, which is also featured in the Little League Museum's final exhibit as one exits through the Hall of Excellence. His role further expanded to "Team Host" status in 2015, which also continues to date. His secret to success, unlike so many, is not about the success that arises after following its principles, but rather the sharing of his secret with as many people around him as possible. His reason for doing this is very simple: "If you help to build up those around you, those around you will continue to build you up." For over 20 years, he has adopted this team-first philosophy in every phase of his life – his coaching, his personal homelife, and his sales management career. This philosophy, he claims, has made all the difference in the world. He is bettered by his wife, TC, and their

40 years of marriage; two sons, Michael and Robert; three grandchildren; and the hundreds of kids and young adults who still refer to him as "Coach Chuck."

Marlin was Chuck's uncle back in 2002 when his team from North Carolina represented the Southeast in the Little League World Series. Since that time, the two men had kept in touch over the years, and in 2014 word got out that Little League International was looking for another team host. A number of current uncles and aunts submitted names they thought would be the right fit. Marlin called his good friend Chuck to see if he would be interested in being a team host. After some thought and Chuck's wife, TC, echoing the same type of sentiment that Brenda did when Marlin was posed the question, Chuck, fortunately, agreed and was very humbled and honored to be considered. After Marlin submitted Chuck's name to Little League International, a background check and interview followed. The rest is history as these two men have been tied at the hip at the Little League World Series since 2015. There's a 50-week separation between the two, but when mid-August comes and the Little League World Series begins, the two reunite and are inseparable for the next two weeks as each year kindles new friendships and treasured memories for two gentlemen who not only have a love for the game, but also a passion for truly giving back.

*Mark Carter, Evan Satinoff, Uncle Marlin Cromley,
Uncle Chuck DeLuca, and Randy Huth*

LIFE AT THE LITTLE LEAGUE WORLD SERIES

Every morning started off with a wake-up call like none other. I belted out a wide range of animal noises from chickens clucking to monkeys grunting and everything in between; these calls echoed throughout the dormitory as 13 boys rolled, twisted, and turned, some with blankets over their heads to help block out the piercing, but unique, zoo and farm-like sounds. Most every morning we had breakfast at the cafeteria between 7:00 -7:30 a.m. Since we were one of the first teams to arrive in Williamsport, the first full day for our team was going to be an extremely active, fast paced day.

Following breakfast, we headed to the recreation room where the Adidas team was awaiting us. Adidas was the apparel sponsor, so all our gear, including cleats, were Adidas branded. As the Adidas team members called out the boys' names, new, vibrant yellow Southeast jerseys and white pants were handed out. Laid out In Randy's room were black Southeast undershirts, long sleeve undershirts, yellow socks, black belts, black arm sleeves, wristbands, and, of course, the renowned yellow and black Little League hats. Just like last year, our team colors were black and yellow, and the uniforms looked sharp. Unlike our Vandy-like pinstripe uniforms where the players picked out their numbers, the LLWS jersey numbers were by size. Following the exchange of some jersey numbers amongst some of the kids, they were handed a LLWS jacket and got fitted for shiny, new Adidas molded cleats. Anticipation was in the air as 13 smiling boys were in awe of what they were receiving. One by one, the boys put on their uniforms as the pride of the Southeast filled the room. During the uniform fitting, Little League photographers snapped candid pictures of the boys trying on their gear. As one can imagine, this was a common occurrence throughout the LLWS experience in Williamsport. Always trying to provide a play-by-play for our parents, the coaches constantly captured photographs and videos of these priceless behind-the-scenes moments for cherished memories ahead.

We left the recreation room and stylishly walked towards the first outfield hill at Lamade Stadium. Awaiting us were two photographers from Little League International. It was time for our team pictures. As the players and coaches settled in, the background of Lamade Stadium and its stands emerged in the background. This was the first time we got a true look at the legendary field. Each player got his individual picture taken with Lamade in the background, and Mark and I got father-and-son pictures. After multiple rounds of photos, we walked collectively to the media building where Little League officials and the ESPN production crew were awaiting us.

As soon as the team walked into the media building, we all got to sign an oversized baseball bat. This bat was going to be a keepsake for sure as every team would be adding their signatures. It also would be the first of many autographs throughout the LLWS these kids would be giving. In preparation for TV time, each player would be called up to be measured and weighed. Maybe an inch or two extra was given with most of the boys growing their hair out and not getting haircuts in the past several months. The team was split into groups as we spent several hours in the studio and media room. Players and coaches were interviewed by ESPN staffers while others were getting their headshots taken for television and the media guide. The interviewing process was an absolute thrill for the boys as they sat calmly on a couch, confidently replying to questions about their superstitions, nicknames, and their experiences so far. As some boys were getting individual action shots taken by professional photographers, others were in the staging area for the video shoot. It was like we were on the set of an actual movie.

Cameras were in position, the casting crew prepped with the boys, and the director shouted, "Quiet on the set and action," as one by one, each boy stepped up and performed a few acts. From action shots like swinging a bat, or catching a ball, to doing the Griddy dance, these boys were in the spotlight and having a blast. After many takes and a ton of laughs, ESPN edited out the best of the best that would eventually be used on national television in the days to come.

Following the media day, we walked towards the indoor cages. Down by the indoor cages were three practice fields where each of the teams had scheduled times to field and throw. No batting practice was ever allowed on these fields. Across the street from the back entrance of the grounds were additional public diamonds where the teams took batting practice throughout their stay at the Little League world series. There were always two ways for us to get to the practice fields and indoor cages. The first path was a road that many of the teams took when walking down to the practice facilities. To the left of the road was the bullpen area followed by residential homes that surrounded the complex. On the right side of the paved road stood both stadiums, well-manicured landscape, and an empty grassy area, which Little League used for parking during games. The secondary route to get to the practice fields or batting cages was the route we took whenever it was game day since we took batting practice in the indoor cages prior to a game.

As we came through the security gate leading from the International Grove, players descended a steep flight of steps down towards the back of Lamade Stadium. There, players would walk along the outside of the stadium where the concession stands and gift shop were located. This area was always filled with fans of all ages. It was customary to walk through the complex during games so the players could connect with the thousands of fans in attendance that day. Often, they would sign autographs, take pictures with fans, or just say hello to the loads of kids that idolized them.

When we made it to the indoor cages, we were greeted by another one of Little League's main sponsors, Easton Sports. Inside the indoor facility was a makeshift store filled with various Easton baseball gear that the kids would be receiving. It was like being a kid in a candy store for these 13 youngsters as each player received a new Easton helmet, batting gloves, backpack, and ADV 360 bat. These bats had not even been released yet to the public as Easton was letting the teams at the LLWS become the first to use them before they hit the shelves. Lastly, we were provided with a few sets of catching equipment. Unlike last year when the equipment was black in color, this year was a first for Easton as helmets and the catching gear were white. Before each boy walked out with a new Easton ADV 360 bat, they had the opportunity to test out the various sizes by taking some BP in the cages. One by one, the boys took their hacks and tried out a few different sizes. Before we ended our session, an Easton associate captured some video of the boys holding their new bats. This video was going to be used on their Tik-Tok page, so one can imagine that the team was super stoked. As we finished up with the Easton representatives and took some individual pictures with the new gear, the boys made sure they thanked the staff for their generosity and time. This on-going example of good manners and respect became a common theme throughout our stay in Williamsport as we were so grateful for the opportunity to be playing at one of the world's biggest sporting events.

Easton demo day

It had been a fun filled day to say the least. Before heading back to the dorms to change for our first practice, we wanted to capture some pictures at some notable landmarks around Lamade Stadium and Volunteer Stadium. Since it was still so early in the week, and we were one of the first teams on campus, we thought this would be the perfect time to take in these most memorable moments. We lined up the team in front of some of the sights and took some unforgettable pictures. Located near the Lamade Stadium scoreboard, the boys posed in front of the Mighty Casey statue, a 14-foot bronze rendition of the legendary slugger from the iconic baseball poem, "Casey at the Bat." We took pictures of the boys in front of the enlarged LLWS baseball located on Lamade's main concourse and snapped some pictures of the team standing shoulder to shoulder in front of the beautifully landscaped, welcome topiary found in back of the Jonathan Levin Memorial Pavilion. However, some of my favorite team photographs that day were taken in the stands of the iconic Howard J. Lamade Stadium.

Later that day, we had our first practice which turned out to be a great one. We still had several days before our opening game vs. Massachusetts, so our practices were vital in keeping us loose and game ready. No matter the time or place, our team was always looking to compete and have fun. I'll always remember the "catch me if you can" runs the boys did following practices. Not everyone was excited to condition after a two-hour practice, but it brought out the competitiveness of these boys while keeping in tip-top shape as well. It was a long, but very productive day, and the boys were ready to get some sleep. Tomorrow would bring another fun-filled day for the Southeast.

The next day started off as usual with a stop at the dining hall for a well-balanced breakfast. The walk to the dining hall was a short one, but I always enjoyed seeing the boys walk together while sharing stories of the day and night before. After breakfast, we headed to the World of Little League Museum. A short walk from the International Grove, this historic museum was located across the street from Little League International's main office building. As we walked into the museum, we were greeted by its curator and staff and began our walking tour of the museum. We arrived in the early morning, so the museum was empty, and we were the only team receiving the tour at that time. We strolled through the museum, often stopping and reading about the historic artifacts displayed in glass cases. The museum not only told the story of Little League's past, but also how Little League has interconnected with U.S. and world history. Despite its smaller size, the museum was very informative as it featured a healthy mix of authentic Little League heritage, artifacts, interactive activities, and captivating media. I had several favorite exhibits, one of which was the Hall of Excellence. The Little League Hall of Excellence is conducted each year for Little League graduates who have shown a commitment to excellence in their chosen profession and represent the values learned as children in Little League. Enshrinement into the Little League Hall of Excellence is the highest honor that Little League can present. This exhibit is in the sixth inning of the museum and features so many rare artifacts and displays from these iconic Little Leaguers. It was interesting to see not just past baseball Hall of Famers like Cal Ripken, Jr. and Nolan Ryan featured in this exhibit, but also U.S. Presidents, George W. Bush and Joe Biden, amongst other U.S. leaders. There were also famous actors featured, such as Kevin Costner. Krissy Wendell, who was the first girl to start at catcher in a LLWS game and went on to become one of the best women ice hockey players in U.S. history, was also honored.

As the three coaches, Uncle Marlin, and Uncle Chuck stopped at each of the exhibits to read and learn more about Little League history, one can imagine what the boys gravitated to. The museum also had some interactive activities, one of which was the boys' favorite. One by one, the boys lined up and sprinted down the line as if they were running out a base hit. Of course, it was timed, and their times were displayed on the wall, so the competitive juices were flowing. Despite spending a lot of time running sprints and disputing who was the faster player, the boys did learn a lot and even got to watch a highlight video of the 2021 LLWS where some past Nolensville Little Leaguers were shown. It was a fun morning filled with baseball, history, and togetherness.

After another light practice, Randy and I headed off campus with Uncle Marlin to visit a really special place. Last year at the LLWS, there were strict guidelines due to COVID-19 for players and coaches to stay on the grounds of the International Grove. This year was different, and although our players didn't leave campus until later into the stay, the coaches made some trips along the way. Randy, Uncle Marlin, and I were heading to West Fourth Street, about 10 minutes down the road from the Little League headquarters. This is where the Carl E. Stotz Field, the birthplace of Little League Baseball, is located. In August of 1938, Carl

E. Stotz, the founder of Little League, brought ten boys aged nine to twelve to this very site. They proceeded to lay out dimensions for a baseball diamond suitable for youth their age. The bases were newspapers, the distance between them was determined by the boys running, and the time between them gauged by a stopwatch. Sixty feet was ultimately the distance selected; 46 feet from the pitcher's mound to home plate was also established. The following year, Carl Stotz started the basis for Little League Baseball by creating a small league of three teams in which children were able to play organized baseball using his new field metrics. That year those three teams played a total of 24 games. However, during the first three years of the league, construction at Williamsport's Memorial Park forced the teams to play at alternative locations. Upon wrapping up the construction in 1942, the small league began playing at the Original Little League field consistently. This original field served as the site of Little League Baseball and hosted the first 12 LLWS (1947-1958).

Despite the field not being used consistently today, it still possesses such charm and beauty. Throughout the park are various statues, plaques, and signs representing Little League baseball and the iconic and innovative Stotz. For 45 minutes, Uncle Marlin, Randy, and I walked these sacred grounds in awe. For Randy, Little League has been part of his DNA for decades. As I walked the park, I could only smile to see Randy, reliving these moments as "his glory days" in the years to come.

Randy and me in front of Carl E. Stotz Field

After spending such special time at the original Little League field, we made one last stop at the corner of Williamsport's Market Square where a few notable bronze statues stand. The batter represents the current player about to hit a game-winning home run. The catcher signifies the Charleston, South Carolina team of all-black youth that were discriminated against in the South in 1955. The umpire, dressed in gear of the 1940's and 1950's, represents the countless number of volunteers who have given their time to the Little League program. There's even a statue of Little League founder, Carl E. Stotz, sitting on a bench. Next to him on the bench one can read the roster that contains the number of the players on the team he managed in 1939. Amongst the other most unforgettable pictures taken of both Randy and me at the original field, we both had to get a snapshot of each of us sitting next to the founder of Little League baseball. Since we were not able to visit this notable site last year, I was thrilled that Randy and I (and, eventually, Mark) were able to witness baseball history.

Fortunately, for Randy and me, Mark was nice enough to stay back with the boys and take his turn visiting this sacred location later in the trip. The boys stayed occupied lounging in the recreation room, while others hung out in the dorms. Mark, on the other hand, continued to provide his daily updates to the parents via the GroupMe app. From the start, we used this app for all team communications. It was and still is to this day such a wonderful means for parents to connect with each other. Throughout the LLWS journey, the pictures and videos we captured of the team and events were posted on GroupMe so the parents could keep up with us. Mark's entertaining commentary of the day's events often provided a ton of laughs as parents (and coaches) read on. Two of my favorite MO's (Mark's Observations) were when he told the parents that the boys were swimming, and Wendy Peffercorn was down there with them. *The Sandlot* lifeguard reference brought many enjoyable comments and giggles, none better than the pun of our lady's man, Lane Dever, trying to get the lifeguard's phone number. Also, signing an autograph was a skill that these boys had not really attempted prior to LLWS, so when Mark noticed a bunch of the boys practicing their signatures on paper, he had to post a comment on GroupMe saying, "Apparently, they don't teach cursive in school anymore." The play-by-play by Mark that he forwarded on this app provided a lot of fun for the parents as well as comfort that their boys were doing just fine.

After the boys finished breakfast the next morning, we had some down time before our practice at the fields. Early mornings in Williamsport brought crisp temps as it usually was in the mid 50's. However, the colder temps never got in the way of an early morning wiffle ball game in the bullpen. It was really fun to see the bond these boys had built both on and off the field. Whether it was playing wiffle ball or ping pong games in the rec room, the friendly competition between them never wavered. Some of our parents had already arrived in Williamsport as the highly anticipated parade was the next day. Other families were traveling out in the next day or two. One thing was for sure, our Nolensville Little League families were ready and anxious to see their kids perform on the world's largest, youth sports stage.

To keep the boys conditioned, later that day we did some training as one by one the boys trotted up the Volunteer Stadium bleacher stairs. Those stairs became a familiar site for me in the days to come. After 30 minutes of some tough, but well-needed conditioning, we headed back to Lamade Stadium where we had the team sit behind home plate. As they got comfortable in their seats, chatting to each other wondering what was next, I told them to close their eyes. The boys, with their eyes closed, were now told to visualize what they were going to do in the days to come to help this team win. It was a visualization exercise that Mark had recommended, and it turned out to be another highlight for the boys, parents, and us coaches. I videoed the boys one by one with my iPhone and asked them what they envisioned. For most, they visualized hitting a walk-off hit, making an incredible defensive play, or having a dominant pitching performance. One player visualized nothing about his on-the-field performance; rather, he envisioned himself cheering his team on from the dugout. Lane Dever's selfless response was all about what we've preached from day one, and that's unity and team. All the kids' answers were awesome, but Lane's response was one that will always stick out.

As the day continued, so did more baseball as we headed to the indoor cages for some early evening batting practice. At this point of the ride, both Mark's and my arms felt robotic-like and were pretty much immune to getting sore based on how much batting practice we had thrown through the weeks. Add on the pure adrenaline of actually being at the LLWS, we just kept throwing and throwing.

Following another enjoyable dinner, the boys made it back to the room to hang out for the night. Just like in days past, we ensured teeth were brushed, boys were showered, and the room was neat and orderly... well, I must admit, the room being tidy was definitely the biggest challenge throughout the stay. Before the lights went out and phones were shut off or silenced, we often played some fun games. Whether it was trivia, offering up a ton of different topics like baseball, football, candy, and animals, or finding out who our best – or possibly worst – spellers were with a good ole fashion spelling bee, or some story time with an imaginary friend named "E-gone"; these boys and coaches had a ton of fun together from early morning wake-up calls to end-of-night entertainment.

PARADE OF THE AGES

The routine of early morning wake-up calls, breakfast, and practice continued as August 15th was going to be such a memorable day. For the last two years, the Grand Slam Parade had been cancelled due to COVID-19. However, today was once again the day when the streets of downtown Williamsport would be filled with tens of thousands of passionate baseball fans stemming from young Little Leaguers to grandparents and everyone in between. Before the 16th annual Grand Slam Parade took place, all 20 teams and umpires were invited to attend the Little League picnic hosted by the Pennsylvania College of Technology. As we loaded up the buses and drove to the college, the enthusiasm began to grow as not only were we going to eat lunch with the other 19 teams, but also the grand marshal of the Grand Slam Parade was going to be talking to the teams. The grand marshal this year was New York Yankee legend and baseball Hall of Famer, Mariano Rivera.

When we arrived at the college campus, we were greeted by college officials and escorted to the tent area where hamburgers and hot dogs were being served for lunch. Each team was accompanied by one of Penn College's softball players. Skyelar, a sophomore outfielder, made sure we felt welcomed throughout the day as she escorted the team throughout the festivities. Following lunch and on-going conversations with some other teams and umpires, we took our seats in front of the podium as the "Sandman" was introduced to the teams by the college's president. Mo's speech to the kids was genuine and direct from the heart. The 13-time all-star and five-time World Series champion told the Little Leaguers how important it was to respect the game of baseball and each other. He emphasized the importance of playing with passion and being the best that they could be. Mariano also spoke about the meaning of playing for one's country and the great game of baseball. As I looked on, watching Mariano talk so eloquently, I also noticed the admiration these kids had for the Hall of Famer. However, no other team was as mesmerized as the Little Leaguers from Panama. Raised in the quiet Panamanian fishing village of Puerto Caimito, Rivera was an amateur player until he was signed by the Yankees organization in 1990. For these Panamanian Little Leaguers and their coaches, Mo was iconic, larger than life. Seeing this team, smiling with so much emotion, was a really special scene. As Mariano finished his speech, and the crowd erupted with applause, each team proceeded to get a team picture with the legendary closer.

Before we lined up to get a few quick pictures, Uncle Marlin asked if I could try to get Rivera's autograph on a baseball. Of course, I obliged, as I knew how Uncle Marlin not only collected Hall of Fame baseballs, but also, notably, he was known to donate such balls for various fundraisers in the future. After we took a couple of priceless snapshots and shook the hand of the baseball great, I pulled out the MLB baseball and asked if I could get a quick signature. I don't think autographs were totally welcomed that day, but it was for Uncle Marlin, so I went to bat for him. With a grin on his face, and a slight hesitation, he inscribed his renowned signature right on the sweet spot. Uncle Marlin was thrilled and for all that he and Uncle Chuck meant to our team, that was the least I could do for him.

We then headed to a downtown Williamsport parking lot where 20 semi-trucks filled their trailer beds with players from around the world. Each team had its own dedicated stage decorated in its country's or region's colors. The boys, one by one, anxiously stepped up onto the trailer bed and got ready for the parade of a lifetime. The trailer bed across from ours was packed with the Australian team and coaches, and they excitedly chanted, "Aussie, Aussie, Aussie... Oy, Oy, Oy!"

There was so much anticipation within the city since this was the first parade in over two years. The Grand Slam Parade was like Little League's version of the opening ceremonies at the Olympics. The floats traveled from Susquehanna St. to Fourth St. and ended at Market Street. Included in the parade were marching bands, antique cars, fire trucks, and more. For the next hour or so, our team and the 19 others were the center of attention. Our boys, proudly waving at the mobs of spectators, also tossed out squishy balls to the children on both sides of the street.

As we continued to cruise around downtown Williamsport, more and more eyes gravitated to the Southeast float. Our boys, coaches, and uncles were having such an incredible time and were soaking up every minute of it. I vividly remember thanking the extraordinary fans for coming out and supporting us. What also struck me was the number of young, passionate baseball players dressed in uniforms that came out that evening to cheer on all these great teams. I shouted, "Keep working hard, and this can be you someday," across the street as I chatted to many young players from the float. I'll never forget the moment when we noticed a mom and her two kids cheering on the Southeast from the side of the road. The older brother, wearing a Southeast shirt and hat, was holding a sign that read "Way to Go." The younger brother, who had just changed out of his Caribbean shirt, was now wearing his Southeast shirt, and waving to the boys. It didn't matter about the team or the country for these enthusiastic fans; all that mattered to them was that the Little League World Series was here and the Grand Slam Parade, which had been cancelled the last two years, was actually happening. Before the parade ended, we were fortunate enough to see some of our families, dressed in black and yellow, in front of City Hall, screaming and waving. All in all, the Grand Slam Parade was one for the ages. This momentous event brought out the beauty of baseball and how it meant so much to the fantastic city of Williamsport and its residents.

Taking in all the excitement at the annual Williamsport Grand Slam Parade

After breakfast the next morning, we headed back to our dorm for another radio interview and a special guest. The Big D and Bubba show, a nationally syndicated morning radio show, played on over 80 country music FM radio stations, wanted to interview Randy and say hello to the team. They had a special guest that morning who wanted to wish the team good luck – none other than country music superstar, Dierks Bentley.

Wednesday, August 17th

The beloved opening day ceremonies and first games of the 2022 Little League World Series were just hours away. After another day of hanging out with the other teams in the rec room, customizing some fun Adidas t-shirts, and refining our swings as we got some final cuts in the batting cages, all our physical and mental preparation for competing at the Little League World Series was about to come into play. Our team was ready. Our families were prepared. Our community was energized. We didn't know, though, if the rest of the nation and entire world was set to see what "We Believe" was all about.

The first game of the 2022 LLWS was an international matchup between Latin America and the Caribbean at 1:00 p.m. EST. All international games were to be played at Volunteer Stadium. The second game of the series, and first U.S. game, was between the Southeast and New England regions. This game was slated for 3:00 p.m. EST at Lamade Stadium. Long lines were already beginning to form outside Volunteer Stadium.

At 11:15 a.m. that morning, however, all 20 teams were participating in the coveted opening ceremonies. This event was essentially an extension of the Grand Slam Parade as it was meant to formally introduce each of the 20 teams. All the teams gathered underneath Volunteer Stadium. Our team was nestled between Mexico and the Midwest region. This event also featured local Pennsylvania District 12 Little Leaguers who displayed flags of the countries participating in this year's tournament. Local dignitaries welcomed the enthusiastic crowd that was flaunting their teams' colors.

As we started to make our way to the left field line, the excitement began to grow. Holding one side of our Southeast Little League Championship banner was Nash; the other side was held by JF. We slowly walked down the left field line proudly waving to our families and others who were cheering, animatedly. All the teams lined up outside on the back edge of the infield grass facing the stadium. During the ceremony, all eyes were glued to the T-Mobile drone while it buzzed through the air taking cool video footage. This epic drone coverage continued throughout the LLWS and followed the teams throughout our stay. One by one, teams were introduced. It was a humbling and thrilling feeling, standing side by side with the best of the best, all 20 Little League teams in the entire world. Following the introductions, all eyes shifted to the jumbotron as a pre-recorded video had players from each team recite lines from the Little League Pledge followed by various coaches reciting the Parent and Volunteer Pledge. The Little League Pledge was written in 1954 by Peter J. McGovern who was the first president of Little League Baseball, Incorporated. Mr. McGovern's goal was to give leagues around the world a pledge displaying some of the thoughts of the Pledge of Allegiance without referencing the United States. He wanted this pledge to include aspects of sportsmanship and the desire to excel. The Little League pledge reads:

I trust in God
I love my country
And will respect its laws
I will play fair
And strive to win
But win or lose
I will always do my best

Since Little League baseball involves so many parents, volunteers, umpires, and much more, Little League decided to craft its own pledge for parents and volunteers as well. The Little League Parent and Volunteer Pledge reads:

I will teach all children to play fair and do their best
I will positively support all managers, coaches, and players
I will respect the decisions of the umpires
I will praise a good effort despite the outcome of the game

Before each LLWS game, following the national anthem, both pledges were recited by a player and coach from the respective teams. The ceremonial first pitches were thrown out by 10 Little Leaguers, while 10 catchers from the other Little League teams participating in the LLWS caught their balls. Jack Rhodes represented the Southeast as he caught a first pitch from a Little Leaguer from Team Mexico. The 20 Little League teams across the globe represented at the 2022 Little League World Series were the following:

- Great Lakes: Hagerstown Little League – Hagerstown, IN

- Metro: Massapequa Coast Little League – Massapequa, NY

- Mid-Atlantic: Hollidaysburg Area Summer Baseball Little League – Hollidaysburg, PA

- Midwest: Davenport Southeast Little League – Davenport, IA

- Mountain: Snow Canyon Little League - Santa Clara, Utah

- New England: Middleboro Little League – Middleboro, MA

- Northwest: Bonney Lake/Sumner Little League - Bonney Lake, WA

- Southeast: Nolensville Little League - Nolensville, TN

- Southwest: Pearland Little League – Pearland, TX

- West: Honolulu Little League – Honolulu, HI

- Asia Pacific: Fu-Lin Little League - Chinese Taipei

- Australia: Brisbane North – Queensland

- Canada: Little Mountain Little League - Vancouver, British Columbia

- Caribbean: Pabao Little League - Willemstad, Curacao

- Europe-Africa: Emilia Romagna Little League - Bologna, Italy

- Japan: Takarazuka Little League - Takarazuka, Hyogo

- Latin America: 14 de Septiembre Little League - Managua, Nicaragua

- Mexico: Matamoros Little League - Matamoros, Tamaulipas

- Panama: Aguadulce Cabezera Little League - Aguadulce, Panama

- Puerto Rico: Guaynabo Baseball Little League – Guaynabo, Puerto Rico

Opening day ceremony introductions at Volunteer Stadium

LAMADE AND VOLUNTEER STADIUMS

When the Little League World Series comes to mind, one would be remiss not to talk about where these Little Leaguers get to play ball. Kids from around the world watching the Little League World Series on ESPN and ABC dream one day to step foot on the hallowed grounds of Lamade and Volunteer Stadiums. When one thinks of youth sports and baseball's most historic stadiums, these two certainly hit the mark. Attendance is always free, and the ambiance is second to none. Built in 1959, Lamade Stadium has a seating capacity of around 45,000. This includes the adjoining hills beyond the outfield fence where kids and adults of all ages enjoy sliding down the iconic hill, hoping not to wipe out on their flattened cardboard boxes. Back in 1992, lights were added; in 2006 additional renovations took place as the fences were moved back 20 feet to 225 ft. to all fields, and some bleachers were replaced with individual seats with backs to increase seating capacity.

The views of Lamade Stadium, with Bald Eagle Mountain as its backdrop, are immeasurable. Surrounded by bright blue skies, the emerald-green sod and the unblemished, infield dirt reminded me of a Major League stadium. Back in 1999, Sports Illustrated chose the top 20 venues of the century to watch a sporting event. No surprise to many, Lamade Stadium made that list and was ranked 16th among the other notables named: Yankee Stadium, Augusta National, Michie

Stadium, Cameron Indoor Stadium, Norway's Bislett Stadium, Wrigley Field, Roland Garros, Lambeau Field, Fenway Park, Saratoga Racecourse, Pebble Beach, Wembley Stadium, Albuquerque's The Pit, Boston Marathon Course, Camden Yards, Lamade Stadium, Daytona International Speedway, Notre Dame Stadium, St. Andrews, and the Rose Bowl.

The stadium adjacent to Lamade is Volunteer Stadium. Constructed in 2001, Volunteer Stadium is where the international tournament is played and is also the home to the annual Little League Challenger Division Exhibition game. Despite not having the legendary hills in the background, Volunteer Stadium still possesses elegant and pristine playing conditions like Lamade Stadium. Within the complex where both stadiums rest are concession stands filled with some of baseball's favorite foods, which are consumed by the thousands of fans that partake in the Little League World Series.

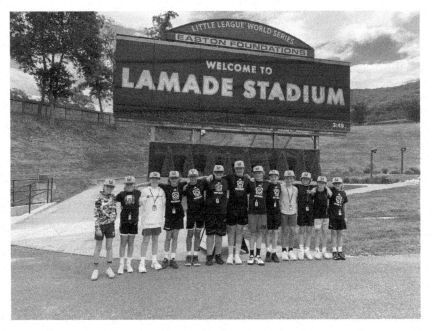

Team picture in front of the jumbo Lamade Stadium sign

LIGHTS, CAMERA, ACTION - ESPN AND ABC

The Little League World Series has been receiving television coverage for the last 50 plus years. In 1953, the LLWS was televised for the first time by CBS. Eventually ABC took over the broadcast rights and has televised LLWS games since 1963, the second-longest deal between a network and event, trailing only the Masters on CBS, which dates back to 1956. While broadcast on ABC, it aired during the weekends under the ABC Wide World of Sports umbrella. In the mid 1980's, Entertainment and Sports Programming Network (ESPN) expanded their global network coverage of the LLWS. In 2001, ESPN covered all eight U.S. regional championship games. The opening of Volunteer Stadium allowed the broadcasting of games to take place simultaneously. In addition, the U.S. Championship game was broadcast live on ABC that year. Today, ESPN and ABC cover all the regional and LLWS games live on their multitude of various brands.

The partnership Little League has formed with ESPN has also garnered a financial boon. Back in 2013, Little League and ESPN struck a deal that paid the organization roughly $7.5 million annually through this year, according to the Sports Business Journal. In 2020, the sides agreed to extend their agreement through 2030.

Over the years, the LLWS had been announced by legendary sportscasters, such as Al Michaels and Brent Musburger. The LLWS and television audiences around the world watched color commentators, such as major league baseball Hall of Famers – Mickey Mantle, Johnny Bench, Jim Palmer, and Tony Gwynn. Since 2006, ESPN's Karl Ravech has provided commentary at the Little League World Series. Joined in this year's U.S. broadcast booth was Kyle Peterson, former MLB player, who had been covering the LLWS since 2003, and two-time Olympic softball medalist, Jessica Mendoza. ESPN analyst, writer, and baseball Hall of Famer, Tim Kurkjian, also filled in a few times in the booth. Two-time Olympic soccer gold medalist, Julie Foudy, provided all the interviews and back stories with players, coaches, and parents throughout the LLWS coverage. All the ESPN announcers, reporters, and staff made the LLWS experience even more unforgettable. From Julie Foudy's pre-game chats with our players to her live TV interviews with many of our parents during the game, the interaction between the ESPN personalities and all the Little Leaguers, coaches, and parents was mind-boggling.

As I think back to all the ESPN personality interactions throughout our journey at the LLWS, a few unforgettable moments come to mind. During some of our rain delays, Kyle Peterson and Jessica Mendoza came down to our dugout to "hangout" with the team. Before games, Tim Kurkjian and Karl Ravech would make it down to the field to chat with the coaches. Always trying to get some insights, Tim Kurkjian actually used some of the feedback on the TV broadcast that we had given during our conversation. All the ESPN personalities and their staff made these Little Leaguers, coaches, and parents feel so welcomed and special.

One of many team meals at our cabin during the state championship

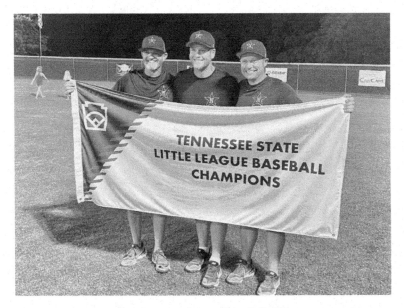

Just three coaches and friends for life

Southeast Champions in front of our hotel in Warner Robins with
our biggest fans behind us

Post game talk at the Little League World Series

William Satinoff and Jack Rhodes
Two of only 40+ in U.S. LLWS history to participate in two LLWS

Coach Mark Carter with his son Nash

Team picture with baseball Hall of Famer – Mariano Rivera

Team picture with baseball superstar and Little League World Series alum – Todd Frazier

Team picture with baseball Hall of Famer – Ferguson Jenkins

Team picture with Little League World Series icon – Mo'ne Davis

Governor Bill Lee talking to the team at the Tennessee State Capitol

Recognition at a Tennessee Titans game

Southeast Champions visiting Bristol Motor Speedway and NASCAR superstar – Austin Dillon (who ironically played on Uncle Chuck's 2002 LLWS North Carolina team)

WE DIDN'T COME THIS FAR, TO ONLY COME THIS FAR

Wednesday, August 17th

Our first game of the tournament had finally arrived. The New England region represented by Middleboro Little League in Middleboro, Massachusetts, was our first opponent of the tournament. What made this opening tournament game even more noteworthy was the history that was about to take place with two of the umpires calling our game. Overall, 16 volunteer umpires made their way from around the world to Williamsport to take part in the 75th LLWS. Andrea Galiano of Ft. Lauderdale, Florida, and the Southeast region would make history as she and her husband, Mike, became the first husband and wife to umpire in the LLWS. Mike was also fortunate enough to have umpired in the 2009 LLWS. The second piece of history came by means of Blake Taylor who was the first British-born umpire at the Little League World Series. We, personally, witnessed history in the making as Andrea umped first base and Blake was behind the plate for our opening game vs. New England.

Unfortunately, our game didn't start on time as there was lightning in the area which caused a one-hour weather delay. After the starting lineups were announced and the national anthem performed, all eyes were going to be on the initial U.S. Little League World Series game of 2022. The first pitch was 74 degrees and overcast, and despite a single by Jack, followed by a double to left field by Bo, two runners were left stranded heading into the bottom of the first. T-Rex, who ended up being one of our most consistent arms throughout the entire LLWS run, toed the rubber for the Southeast. After giving up a lead-off walk, Trent induced a fielder's choice followed up by a strikeout. Then, with a runner on second, Sati made what turned out to be a top 10 play on Sportscenter that night as he sprawled out, dove to his backhand side, and threw the batter out from his knees saving a potential run. As the third out was called, the team ran to the dugout after that breathtaking play and was met by the rest of the players outside the dugout waiting to rejoice a stellar first inning of the LLWS.

The momentum continued in the top of the second inning when Nash started us off with a lead-off walk. After moving over on a passed ball, Josiah followed with a good AB by advancing Nash to third with a fly ball to right field. One batter later with two outs, Caz Logue was called upon to pinch hit for Grayson May and delivered a gritty base on balls. With two outs, runners on first and third, William stepped to the plate, and on a 0-1 count, delivered a ground ball base hit, right by the stretched-out third baseman, bringing home Nash for our first run of the game.

After a scoreless bottom half of the second inning for New England, our bats began to get hot in the third. After Bo walked, Wright took one for the team and got drilled in the side by a scorching fastball. Drew Chadwick followed with a hard-hit, ground ball base knock past the diving third baseman. After a JF strikeout, Josiah launched a towering fly ball over the leftfielder's head for a long single scoring Bo and Wright. Then, with two outs, Grayson worked the count for a walk, loading the bases. Back to the top was William, and on a full count, Sati hit a hard, line drive right up the middle scoring both Drew and Josiah. Heading into the bottom of the third, the Southeast took a commanding 5-0 lead. Nevertheless, nothing could be taken for granted as we knew this New England team was scrappy and had the bats to come back at any time. In the bottom of the third, they did just that, scoring two runs and cutting the lead to three.

After a scoreless top of the fourth inning, New England put together three consecutive singles vs. T-Rex to load the bases. Out to the mound Randy strolled to make a pitching change. Trent had pitched one heck of a game, and we were now turning it over to our 11-year-old ace, Nash Carter, to close the door. With one out, Nash induced a ground ball to William who tried turning a 6-4-3 double play with Lane, but the runner at first just beat the throw and New England's third run crossed the dish. After a base on balls to load the bases, up stepped New England's most feared hitter. On the first pitch, a hanging breaking ball, their lead-off batter smashed an absolute seed down the third base line only to be caught by Chadwick. They don't call it the hot corner for nothing as Drew's dramatic grab saved two potential runs.

Unfortunately, the bad weather reappeared, and the second weather delay of the game occurred. The sensational grounds crew, who for the most part was made up of volunteers across the country, quickly tarped the diamond and both teams began to wait patiently in their dugouts. During the 2 ½ hour rain delay, we ended up in the media room where post-game interviews took place. Fortunately, some of our awesome parents brought us some food to snack on as the boys were getting hungry. The weather wasn't letting up, and the delay trickled on, but the good news was some trivia and small talk amongst our team kept things loose.

7:13 p.m. EST arrived and it was time to resume the game with Southeast leading New England 5-3 heading into the top of the fifth. After a leadoff walk to pinch hitter, Charlie Malom, the New England pitcher bore down and set the next three batters in order. Nash returned to the mound in the bottom of the fifth inning, and someone in centerfield became extra busy. After Nash induced a fly ball to centerfield for the first out, a bona fide web-gem followed as Grayson May dove headfirst, laying out on the wet grass making one spectacular play for the second out of the inning. This play and title of "Mullet Superman" would end up going viral as it made its way on ESPN.com, Barstool Sports, and other media outlets. Nash ended the fifth by getting his first "K" of the LLWS.

The top of the sixth brought more offense as William led off the inning with another base knock, followed by Jack's double to right field. After two consecutive outs and Drew's base on balls, up stepped Carter. With the bases loaded and Nash looking to help his own cause, a floating line drive was snarled by the shortstop. Although we didn't capitalize with men on second and third and none out, we knew, heading into the bottom of the sixth inning, the importance of getting the first out of the inning. Carter continued his dominance as he punched out back-to-back batters and yielded yet another fly ball out to none other than "Mullet Superman." Ball game!

In front of a crowd of 9,173 fans, and many more, including those back home, watching live on ESPN, we got our first "W" of the LLWS under our belt. We Believe. What was even more impressive with this victory was that regardless of the gigantic crowd, bright lights, cameras, and global spotlight, these boys played with the utmost composure, confidence, and grace. Even though only William and Jack played here the previous year, albeit in front of a much smaller crowd, our first game in 2022 felt somewhat routine. The offense was led by William with three hits and three RBI's, Jack added another two base knocks, and "Big Hand Joe" drove in two runs. T-Rex roared right through the New England line up surrendering three earned runs and striking out four in 3 1/3 innings, and Nash slammed the door pitching a flawless 2 2/3 innings, punching out three New England batters. Right from the start when we assembled this team, the three coaches knew how vital and strong our defense would need to be to go deep into the tournament. Our "D" certainly didn't let us down in game one of the LLWS as not only did we play errorless baseball, but also William and Grayson made gold-glove type plays at short and centerfield. We Believe.

After each game the coach and certain players from the winning team are asked by Little League to attend the post-game press conference. The first post-game presser drew Randy, William, Josiah, and Nash to the press room. A small group of media members fired off questions to Randy and the boys. One of the reporters asked William about it being his second time here at the Little League World series and what he learned last year that may be helping him now. Sati responded, cool as a cucumber, as he talked about not getting nervous, staying loose, and just having confidence in defense and on offense. A reporter then asked 11-year-old Nash about his pitching performance and his reply was full of innocence and humility. Nash also talked about the importance of confidence and how he had it in his defense and how the team had it in his pitching. He further explained how he overcame his nervousness by having played in the spotlight and on television during the Southeast Regional the prior month. Josiah was then asked about how it felt getting the big hit early on and, ultimately, the win vs. New England. Confident and composed, Josiah said how amazing it was to get the insurance runs for the team and how it picked the team up.

Later in the presser, Randy was asked about the win. He spoke about how our team was built on a defensive strategy and the importance of having our pitchers fill up the zone. He went on to say how we wanted to win the freebie war every time, which meant not giving up errors and walks, and how if those two things happen, usually the outcome will be in our favor. The Q&A went on for another four minutes or so and included commentary from Randy about the importance of the first win, and what the team did to stay loose during the rain delay. Phrases like "staying loose" and "having fun" were expressed, but also the relevance of knowing that once we got back to the field, we had a job to do. One of the reporters talked about how he thought the team played with such composure and didn't show any apprehension. When asked about it, Randy spoke about last year and how it was the team's first time on the big stage. He went on to talk about the experience we had this year by having two players, William and Jack, who played in last year's LLWS. Having Jack and William tell the others what to expect during the course of the series helped prepare the team in so many ways. After talking more about our pitching depth and who was slated to go for the next game, the presser concluded, and full of smiles and happiness, Randy, Josiah, William, and Nash stepped down from the platform and headed back to the dorms to be greeted with jubilation by their other teammates.

The day following our first ever LLWS win brought much excitement and anticipation for our next game. The buzz around Williamsport was hopping. The front page of the local newspaper, the Williamsport Sun-Gazette, had a picture, captioned "Off and Running," of William and Drew giving a high five to each other. Even more excitement was happening back home. From the Historic Nolensville School's marquee's message, "So Proud of our Nolensville Little League Team," to the many other signs around town wishing the team good luck, there was a vibe back in Nolensville like none other. Many local Middle Tennessee schools also created signs wishing the team good luck while other schools wore black clothing displaying Nolensville spirit throughout the halls. As well, the national and local interviews just kept coming in as many of the boys got interviewed by radio stations throughout Tennessee along with local television news affiliates.

Early that morning before the boys had to be awakened, I headed for my customary walk near the public park where we took outdoor batting practice. There was a walking trail surrounding the ballpark which I strolled for a mile or two each morning. It was super refreshing and tranquil to be outside on those early, brisk mornings. During my walks, I would often reflect on the time we were having at the Little League World Series. Many times, while walking, I would give my parents or brother a call and talk about the prior day's or night's game. As Mark and the boys slept, Randy also escaped the dormitory life and sat on the hill at Lamade Stadium for some reflection of his own. Since we were both early risers, most of the time we were the only two people in or near the stadium.

Later that day, as we walked as a team down the steps leading to the concourse of Lamade Stadium, we stopped at the oversized bracket board that was hanging near the gift shop. As teams won or, unfortunately, lost, the bracket board would continuously be updated. Just above the Mountain sign, a bold yellow rectangular sign read "Southeast." It was set. The 10th game of the tournament on Friday, August 19th, at 3:00 p.m. EST would be the Southeast taking on the Mountain region.

It was now practice time, so we headed back to the indoor cages to get more swings in. It became routine at the Little League World Series for Mark to talk to the boys before each cage session. His guidance was always consistent. He often talked about being focused during the 1 ½ hour batting practice session. Although the boys had a ton of fun throughout their stay, we had a lot of work to get done and still had our eye on one thing – Winning the 2022 Little League World Series. It became routine during our indoor batting practice sessions to compete against one another as we broke into two groups. The friendly competition between the boys kept these 13 young men determined and driven.

Later that night we walked back over to Lamade to catch the night cap of the U.S. bracket. When teams were not playing or practicing, many of them ended up at the Lamade or Volunteer stadiums to watch the other games as spectators. At Lamade Stadium seats would be reserved for the other teams' coaches and players down the left field line. That night we watched as the Southwest, represented by Pearland Little League, ended up beating the home state favorites from Hollidaysburg, Pennsylvania, 8-3 in front of a packed house at Lamade. After a late night at Lamade, we headed back to the dorms to get some sleep.

Friday, August 19th

The next day, following a hearty breakfast, Uncle Chuck had a special surprise in store for the team. Uncle Chuck was known for his "walkabouts," and to date the team had not experienced such a thing, so the boys scampered out of the dormitory to meet Uncle Chuck in front of the building. For the next few hours, Uncle Chuck guided the 13 youngsters on a walk around the campus of the Little League complex. From pointing out significant landmarks and introducing the boys to volunteers, to bumping into and taking a picture with legendary Little Leaguer, ex-major league baseball superstar and current ESPN commentator, Todd Frazier, Uncle Chuck kept the boys entertained while the coaches sat back in the dorms and relaxed. One of the most memorable moments from that walkabout was when the boys had the chance to slide down the iconic hill at Lamade Stadium. Whether it was wiping out on their flattened cardboard boxes, taking pictures with young fans, or simply signing an autograph for one of the many Southeast fans in attendance, the notorious Uncle Chuck Walkabout turned out to be a treasured time.

Some of the boys taking turns sliding down the iconic hill at Lamade Stadium

As the day went on, so did our eagerness to get the second game of the LLWS started. We finished up with another solid round of BP in the indoor cages before we made our walk to the stadium. Little did the boys know, walking up from the cages, that on top of the hill were two special guests ready to greet them. Scott and Nolan Brown decided to make the trip from Tennessee to support the 2022 Nolensville All-Star team. Both Nolan, having been there the year before as a participant of the LLWS, and Scott, as a passionate fan, wanted to experience the sights and sounds of what the LLWS was all about without COVID-19 protocols. I had asked both Scott, who is the pitching coach for Vanderbilt University, and Nolan to say a few words of encouragement to the team before they stepped on the field against Utah. It was super exciting to see both these guys in person in Williamsport, and the words that they communicated brought motivation to our team. After some handshakes and pictures with Scott and Nolan, we proceeded to walk into Lamade Stadium.

It was a mostly sunny afternoon with temps in the mid-80's as the Southeast was getting ready to take on the Mountain region in a mid-afternoon matchup at Lamade Stadium. Being the Mountain region's first LLWS game, it was supposed to be a day filled with much excitement and anticipation for the players, coaches, and fans of Snow Canyon Little League from Santa Clara, Utah. Regrettably, earlier that week one of their players was involved in a very unfortunate accident, which left a player in critical condition at a local hospital. Heading into this game, we recognized that there would be a ton of emotion. Knowing the anguish Utah's players, coaches, and fans were going through, we wanted to pay tribute to the young boy who was hospitalized. As we took the field for our phantom infield prior to the start of the game, all our boys and coaches trotted out to the field proudly wearing Mountain region fitted ball caps. Following a flawless phantom infield, we jogged over to the first base dugout and stood in front of the Mountain team and all their fans. Randy gave a brief signal and then we all took off our Mountain hats and tipped them to the team and their fans. This sign of hopefulness and compassion was felt throughout the stadium as the Utah faithful gave our team a standing ovation along with our Southeast fans. Randy then lovingly walked over to one of the coaches and handed him a Southeast hat that all the team had signed. As Randy hugged the coach, who, ironically, was the dad of the boy who got injured, tears flooded the stadium seats. Fortunately, the young man who suffered that heartbreaking injury has recovered well over the last several months.

Then, introductions played over the loudspeaker and the one-off handshakes followed as both teams toed the foul line for the national anthem. Being the visitors, we had first crack to put some runs on the board. The top of the first started with a leadoff walk by Satinoff, followed by a line drive by Rhodes to left field. The two table setters were now onboard, and with one out, Wright Martin hit a flaring line drive for an infield hit. Drew Chadwick stepped up with the bases loaded and worked a base on balls scoring William for the first run of the game. Then, on the first pitch, Nash Carter delivered with a clutch, stand-up double that landed just over third base scoring both Jack and Wright to up the lead to three. Josiah Porter walked on another full count, and Caz Logue then strutted to the batter's box with the bases juiced. On a 1-1 count, Caz launched a towering fly ball that just kept traveling. The Mountain centerfielder drifted back near the warning track, initially lost the ball, but rebounded to make the second out of the inning. It was a productive at bat for Logue as he drove in the fourth run of the inning, and it was a very productive top of the first with nine batters stepping to the plate and four runs scoring. We decided to throw Drew Chadwick vs. Utah and he did not disappoint. He started the bottom of the first with two consecutive ground ball outs. With two outs, Utah's third batter stepped up to the plate and delivered a single to right field giving him Utah's first ever LLWS hit. A double to left over Josiah's head scored the Mountain region's first run of the game and tournament, and heading into the top of the second, the score was 4-1 Southeast.

The top of the second started off like the first inning with Sati drawing a walk followed up by a sharp, line-drive double by Jack & Cheese. Due to some aggressive third base coaching by some guy named Evan Satinoff, William was thrown out by the centerfielder on a bang-bang play. A wild pitch advanced Jack to third base; then, Bo Daniel got drilled right in the back. With men on first and third, Wright Martin stepped up to the plate. The young Utah hurler had a hard time finding the zone as Jack Rhodes made it 5-1 after scoring on a wild pitch. Bo, ultimately, advanced to third base on another wild pitch, and on a 2-2 count, Wright struck out swinging but moved ahead to first on a dropped third strike, leading Bo to score from third as well. The inning finally ended, but not without another two runs scoring. Now, in the bottom of the second inning, the Southeast was leading the Mountain region by a score of 6-1. The bottom of the second brought more strikes and outs as Drewbie mowed down the next three batters, 1-2-3. The third inning went by quickly while both pitchers induced 1-2-3 consecutive half innings.

It was in the top of the fourth inning that our offense stalled. Other than Jack Rhodes' second double of the game and third hit overall, our bats started to cool off. Chadwick strolled back out to the mound in the bottom of the fourth inning and got into a little trouble by hitting the first batter. Little League baseball is built around sportsmanship, and throughout the post season, when one of our pitchers hit a batter, immediately, they trotted to first base to see if the batter was all right. This gamesmanship continued at the LLWS when "Mountain Drew" casually jogged to the bag to check up on the hit batsman. Now, with one out and runners on first and third, Utah pulled off a double steal as another run crossed the plate. After Drew got into a little bit of a jam with runners now on first and third, and his pitch count on the rise, we decided to bring in William to relieve Chadwick. Following Sati's first pitch of the inning, Utah decided to attempt another double steal, but, fortunately for us, it was beautifully thwarted as Jack threw a rocket down to Nash at second base and eventually Wright was able to tag the runner before the player on third crossed home plate. The successful execution of this defensive gem was extremely rewarding to see since it was something we had worked on in practices all summer long.

The top of the fifth inning started off when JF Forni legged out an infield single. Caz, batting for Lane Dever, came up next and laced a line drive single to right. With runners on first and second and none out, Grayson May stepped to the plate. Despite bunting not being one of this team's stronger traits, I gave Grayson the sacrifice bunt sign as we needed to move the runners over. On the first pitch, May squared around to bunt the ball, missed, but, fortunately, the catcher couldn't handle the pitch and runners advanced to second and third. Despite not getting the bunt down, Grayson's at bat still was a success. The very next pitch skipped by the catcher as Grayson took a cut, sending the ball to the backstop. JF sprinted home, sliding in safely for our seventh run of the game. As the pitcher covered the plate, the ball got by him and Lane, pinch running, who had never stopped sprinting from second base came dashing home, sliding safely for our eighth run. Throughout the summer, we coaches continued to talk about the importance of hustling. This baserunning example, which was one of my favorites throughout the summer, not only showcased tremendous hustle, but also, importantly, displayed superb baseball instincts from Lane. Back to the top of the order with one out, William hit a hard ground ball up the middle for a base knock. After another wild pitch advanced Sati to second, Jack came up and crushed a line-drive single to right giving him a total of four hits for the day. Next, Bo Daniel came to the plate with runners on second and third and another wild pitch ensued, scoring William with the ninth run of the game. After a walk to Bo, Wright came up and sent a long, towering fly ball to left field scoring Jack on a sacrifice fly. With two outs, Chadwick came through once again with a single falling right in front of the left fielder, scoring Bo-Bo with the eleventh run of the game. The inning just kept going when T-Rex hit a scorcher to right field advancing Drew to third base.

As the throw came into third, Trent hustled to second only to be thrown out for the third out of the inning. It was a super productive top of the fifth inning as the Southeast erupted for five runs to take a commanding 11-2 lead going into the bottom of the fifth. Pitching ruled the next inning and a half as no runs came across for either team. It was now the bottom of the sixth with two outs when Grayson May called, "Ball! Ball! Ball!" and secured the final out of the game.

In front of a roaring and poignant Lamade Stadium crowd of 10,501, our second game of the LLWS was in the books with another win. We exploded with 12 hits and 11 runs vs. Utah and, unmistakably, the hitting star of the game was Jack Rhodes as he went 4-4 with three runs scored. Drew Chadwick and Nash Carter also added to the hit parade with one base knock a piece, and both drove in two runs. Between Drew and William, the arms from Tennessee quieted the Utah bats by only giving up two hits and one earned run. The defense was stellar and played errorless baseball, again. We Believe.

Following the victory, Randy, Jack, and Drew headed to the press room to answer questions from the various reporters. Right at the start, a reporter from Salt Lake City asked Randy about the relevance of our team wearing the Mountain hats during our phantom infield and going over to their dugout and tipping our caps to their team and fans. Randy eloquently talked about the emotion that had been built up for Utah following the heart-wrenching incident that took place with one of their players. He went on to say that, yes, we were going to play baseball and be competitive; however, we still had compassion for the Utah team and were thinking about them and keeping them in our thoughts. A question was also posed about our phantom infield and how it got started. Randy told the story about how it originated. The conversation about the phantom infield brought giggles from Jack and Drew. Jack & Cheese talked about how the phantom infield brought him confidence knowing that he couldn't make an error. Drew, on the other hand, talked about how it made him feel really flashy and cool in front of all the fans. Regardless of how it looked, all the boys thought this pre-game routine was extremely fun. Jack was also asked about how it felt making it back to the LLWS. He went on to say that he felt like one of the veterans and liked helping prepare his teammates as to what to expect. It was so refreshing to hear Jack talk about the experience at the LLWS. Jack said, "You got to act like no one is there and play your hardest and play your best because this is a once in a lifetime opportunity." When Drew was asked about how he felt on the mound that day, he answered the question like a seasoned pro. He talked about the word which was commonly used throughout our LLWS journey: confidence. Drew, who started that game, talked about when he was taken out of the game and the tons of faith he had in Sati to end the game. The response Drew gave again showed the selflessness these 13 players had towards each other. Everyone believed in each other, and the confidence each player possessed was becoming contagious. Jack was then asked about his 4-4 game and how he felt. There was no surprise that confidence was the name of the game. Jack talked about how he didn't think about how he could go 4-4, rather he was focused on the next at bat and what's coming next. He didn't care about the last at bat, good or bad, but rather he concentrated on his next at bat and how he could help the team win. Hearing the response from Jack, one would have thought he was an MLB veteran rather than a 12-year-old Little Leaguer.

Later that night, most of the team headed back to Lamade Stadium to watch a powerhouse matchup between the West Region, represented by Hawaii, and New York, represented by the newly formed Metro region. The team from Hawaii had already defeated the Northwest Region by a score of 11-1 on Wednesday night and was already being considered the favorite by so many to win the 2022 Little League World Series. Hawaii kept up its dominance as they overpowered and shut out the strong Metro team from New York by a score of 12-0. It was always an enjoyable time for the team to make it back to games later in the evening. Whether they munched on some of the delicious concession foods and watched the game from the left field line or walked aimlessly around the stadium grounds, the boys were soaking up every minute they were at the LLWS.

There were a few key takeaways heading into the busy weekend. First, since we went 2-0 in our first two games, we weren't going to play any games over the weekend. Next up for us was the U.S. quarterfinals on Monday, August 22nd vs. a determined Great Lakes team from Indiana who had previously won a thriller against Iowa from the Midwest region, so we had a couple days rest ahead of us. This was awfully important for our pitchers so they could rest their arms and be ready to go on Monday. However, despite not playing any games, we still had a lot of preparation to get done while practicing at the public park across the street and indoor cages.

All throughout our stay we received special messages, gifts, and more from a variety of different businesses and organizations from back home. Although the team was entirely unaware, one of Nolensville's finest flew up to Pennsylvania to come watch us play vs. Utah. Nolensville's Police Chief Roddy Parker and a friend made the trek from back home to root their home team on and experience the LLWS in person. Unfortunately, we did not have the opportunity to visit with the chief, but he was gracious enough to leave some tokens of good luck and appreciation with our team. Chief Parker brought black Nolensville Police hats and a one-of-a-kind Nolensville Police coin for each of our players and coaches.

The team showing off their Nolensville Police hats and one-of-a-kind coins

Also, earlier in the week, I found out that former Baseball Hall of Fame President, Jeff Idelson, was going to be paying a visit to Williamsport. Jeff, now the co-founder of Grassroots Baseball, and Jean Fruth, the other co-founder of

Grassroots Baseball, were going to do a book signing for their recent book, *Grassroots Baseball Route 66,* on Saturday afternoon. The event, a fundraiser for Little League Baseball, also featured Baseball Hall of Fame pitcher, Ferguson Jenkins. The newly published *Grassroots Baseball Route 66* book was being sold, and Jeff, Jean, and Fergie would be signing autographs and taking pictures with fans. Once I found out Jeff was visiting the Little League World Series, I reached out to him and scheduled some time to swing by their tent to say hello. Jeff, who had been with the Baseball Hall of Fame for over 25 years, was a friend of the family for many years. Back in 2007 and 2008, my father; my brother, Dan; my cousin, Andrew; and I attended the Baseball Hall of Fame Fantasy Camp where we got to know Jeff. Our friendship had continued throughout the years, and it was a joy to spend a few minutes with him, especially during the Little League World Series. Once I knew Fergie Jenkins was attending the book signing, I told the team, and they came down to meet the all-time great and get a picture with him.

Later that day, I recall reaching out via GroupMe to the parents asking for a snack drop. Our parents were always so accommodating and helpful. Within a few hours some of the boys' favorite snacks – Cheez-It, Slim Jim, beef jerky, Gushers, Skittles, assorted cookies and more – were delivered outside the security gates where we met a few parents for the hand off. Now, our first day off was soon coming to an end. Knowing Sunday was going to be a hectic but super exciting day, we ended the night with some late-night trivia and stories before we shut off the lights and silenced the phones.

Sunday morning started out like every other morning for me at the LLWS. Around 6:00 a.m., I woke up, threw on my navy-blue Rays hoodie, Southeast hat, and LLWS lanyard and headed out for my daily morning walk. As I trotted down the stairs leading to the Lamade Stadium concourse, I made a sharp left turn and immediately walked over to the enlarged white bracket board only to fix my eyes on our next big matchup vs. the Great Lakes. There was a lot of excitement in the air despite this highly anticipated game not taking place for another day.

Following another peaceful, but much needed walk, I headed back to the dorms for the daily wake-up call. We had another little surprise for the boys that morning, this time from the Nashville Predators. The boys made their way to Randy's room where he handed each of them an authentic Nashville Predators jersey, hat, and yellow pair of sunglasses. Those cool shades became somewhat of a favorite apparel item for the kids and coaches as we wore them throughout our time at the LLWS. The overall support we received from local Nashville sports teams and businesses throughout the journey, including the Nashville Sounds, Tennessee Titans, and others was so remarkable and exceedingly generous.

The team was extremely pumped up for Sunday's festivities. Since 2017, Little League International has partnered with Major League Baseball to put on the annual Little League Classic game played at Bowman Field in Williamsport. Not only would all the teams, families, and fans attend this game, but also both MLB participating teams would spend time at Lamade Stadium, watching one of the afternoon games on Sunday and intermingling with the other teams not playing that day. Last year the Angels and Indians played in the MLB Classic. Despite battling COVID-19 protocols, the 2021 team still had the opportunity to hang out with players from each team. Baseball superstars – Mike Trout, Shohei Ohtani, Jose Ramirez, and Triston McKenzie – graced us with their presence as they signed autographs, took pictures, and some even slid down the Lamade Stadium hill. This year's MLB Classic was going to bring two AL East teams to Williamsport: the Baltimore Orioles and Boston Red Sox.

Later that morning the Chinese Taipei, Mexico, Panama, and Southeast teams all met in a parking area behind Volunteer Stadium. Dressed in their white baseball pants, black Southeast undershirts and yellow caps, the team gathered to wait for the Orioles team bus to arrive and were welcomed by various Little League International officials, photographers, and other dignitaries. The boys, who were getting a bit antsy to meet the players, had fun mingling with the other Little Leaguers.

I, on the other hand, spotted from a distance a somewhat distinguished MLB figure – the Commissioner of Baseball, Rob Manfred. The Commish had been in this illustrious role since 2015 when he succeeded Bud Selig and during his time has been the centerpiece amongst many controversies. Last year, I had the opportunity to speak with him at Lamade Stadium during a game and, passionately, told him that the city of Nashville needed an MLB franchise. As I gathered my thoughts and hinted to Mark Carter what I was about to do, I casually walked over to Commissioner Manfred, re-introduced myself, shook hands, and began my conversation. Although I could have brought my many opposing viewpoints, I didn't; I wanted to have a somewhat respectful chat with him. No different from last year, I brought up the city of Nashville and how they are determined to get an MLB team. Following my desperate, but rather fiery, pitch for baseball in the Music City, he proceeded to say that before baseball comes to Nashville, the stadium situation for both the A's and Ray's needed to get rectified. As a diehard Rays fan, I certainly knew where he was coming from, but the fact that he acknowledged Nashville for a potential MLB destination really made my Sunday morning.

A few minutes after my brief, but friendly, conversation with Manfred, I noticed a lot of the boys hovering around a young, striking, African American woman dressed in black. It was none other than Little League legend, Mo'ne Davis. Hailing from Taney Little League out of Philadelphia, Pennsylvania, Mo'ne and her Mid-Atlantic team played in the 2014 Little League World Series. She was the 18th girl overall to play in the LLWS and the first girl to earn a win and to throw a shutout in Little League World Series history. Davis and her electric 70 MPH fastball shut out Chris Mercado's Southeast – South Nashville Little League by the score of 4-0. Adding to her legacy, Mo'ne became the first Little Leaguer featured on the cover of Sports Illustrated. Mo'ne, now an infielder, currently plays softball for Hampton University. ESPN2 was featuring a KidsCast as an alternate telecast of the Orioles vs. Red Sox game, and Mo'ne was going to be a guest that night. The team had a fantastic conversation with Mo'ne, reminiscing a bit about her glory days, and we couldn't leave without getting a snapshot of her with the team.

Suddenly, we saw from a distance a charter bus heading our way. All the teams that had been patiently waiting for the Orioles to arrive were now yearning with anticipation. Television cameras and photographers from the MLB, Little League International, and other outlets gathered closely around the circle of players waiting for the Orioles grand entrance. At last, the Orioles players and coaches stepped off the charter bus wearing their game jerseys, jeans, and assorted

LLWS team hats. When their feet hit the pavement, the teams immediately gravitated to them with high fives and handshakes. Whether it was some of the Oriole Hispanic players fist bumping Team Mexico and chatting in Spanish or our players taking pictures with MLB super stars, the smiles on all these youngsters' faces was simply amazing. I remember two specific players that really stood out with our team. Outfielder, Austin Hays, talked to many of our players, signed autographs, and even took some pictures. The other Orioles player that our team was immediately attracted to was rookie sensation, Adley Rutschman. The phenomenal young catcher was a juggernaut in college when he had attended Oregon State University, and his superstar status now carried over to the big leagues. As the teams started to make their way down the paved walkway leading to Lamade Stadium, our boys were on Rutschman's heels, following him step by step. For the next few minutes, the Orioles, LLWS teams, security, and media made their way to Lamade Stadium only to be surrounded on each side by feverish fans of all ages trying to seek an autograph, take a quick picture, or just give a high five to one of the Orioles players.

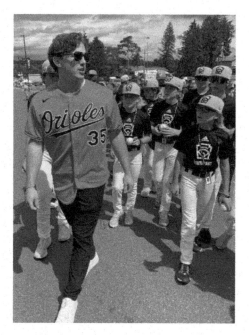

The boys joyfully walking with Orioles superstar Adley Rutschman arriving at Lamade Stadium

Making that grand entrance into the stadium before watching the Midwest take on the Mountain region was a very cool experience for our team. As we walked up the left field bleacher ramp leading into the stadium, we were directed by ushers to take our seats. As the boys sat down on the green stadium seats, they each left a seat open waiting anxiously for the big leaguers to come sit by them. Orioles and Red Sox players started making their entrances into the stadium and the oohs and ahhs erupted throughout the crowd. Some of the players decided to dart to the hill before heading to the stands so they could experience sliding down the iconic Lamade hill. Fortunately, that meant that many of our players' siblings had the opportunity to get autographs and slide down the hill with the big leaguers. For some, getting an autograph or quick picture at a game was the closest they'd ever been to an MLB player; for others, it was their first time seeing a big leaguer up close and personal. For the entire Southeast team, it was undoubtedly the first time they'd had a chance to sit right next to a major leaguer, chat it up, laugh, giggle, and smile from ear to ear, talking about the greatest sport on earth.

Some of my most memorable moments at the LLWS took place that day. It didn't matter that these baseball players had Red Sox stitched on the front of their jerseys or names like Martinez, Devers, Hosmer, or Bogaerts on their backs. No matter their economic status, age, race, or language spoken, all these super-stars, including our own, had one thing in common: love, passion and respect for each other and the game of baseball. Whether it was Grayson May interviewing five-time All-Star, J.D. Martinez, live on ESPN or Trent McNiel talking pitching with flamethrower, Garrett Whitlock, the sights and sounds of the day were simply unforgettable. One of my favorite conversations was one William had with one of the best young players in the game, third baseman and two-time All-Star, Rafael Devers. Sitting right behind Devers, William and Caz, I had a bird's eye view of their entire back and forth conversation. William, being a Tampa Bay Rays fanatic, had to bring up the rivalry between the Red Sox and Rays. His conversation did not disappoint as he went on to emphatically tell the 26-year-old Dominican super star who was the better team. The joshing didn't end there as Sati had to set the record straight on his opinion of Tampa Bay Rays phenom, Wander Franco, being a better shortstop than Dever's current teammate and close friend, Xander

Bogaerts. Despite Bogaerts sitting four seats down from Rafael, I was super proud of my son representing the Rays and his favorite player, Wander. The ribbing between William and his new pal, Rafael, went back and forth for quite a while, bringing huge smiles and laughs between the two.

William and Boston Red Sox All-Star, Rafael Devers, talking all things baseball

The MLB players had to leave early that game since the MLB Little League Classic game was later that night. After the Midwest vs. Mountain game, we headed back to the dorms to relax a little before we departed for the MLB Classic game. I remember William telling me he befriended Devers on Instagram and even sent him an instant message telling him how fun it was talking to him and thanking him for his time. Within a few minutes, Rafael responded, certainly making William's day.

Later that day, all 20 teams took a short 15-minute bus ride to Muncy Bank Ballpark at historic Bowman Field, home to the Williamsport Crosscutters, a collegiate summer baseball team of the MLB Draft League. However, on this night, it wouldn't be hundreds of Little Leaguers from around the globe watching the Crosscutters; rather, these Little League super stars would be watching, up close and personal, a live MLB game between the Baltimore Orioles and Boston Red Sox.

The City of Williamsport didn't just welcome two storied MLB franchises, but also opened their doors to two prominent dignitaries. Earlier that day, former President George W. Bush and the widow of baseball icon, Jackie Robinson, took part in the dedication of the final three, Bases Loaded project statues in downtown Williamsport. The ceremony, which was part of the 75th anniversary of the Little League World Series, unveiled statues of President Bush, Jackie Robinson, and another Hall of Famer, Cy Young, located near one of the other statues of Little League founder, Carl E. Stotz.

Back at Lamade that night, all 20 teams, families, and select fans started packing the small, but mighty, stadium that had a seating capacity of 2,366 fans. All the teams had epic seats with the Southeast sitting in the first couple of rows behind the right of home plate. While sitting down noshing on some snacks the stadium provided, I noticed a special somebody out of the corner of my eye. Low and behold, it was President George W. Bush, flanked by secret service men, 10 feet in front of us on the field. President Bush, who played Little League, and is the only sitting president to have attended the Little League World Series (2001), was chatting it up with some folks on the field and even took a quick snapshot with the LLWS mascot, Dugout. As the President was introduced to the capacity crowd, he waved his hand at the Williamsport faithful.

Right before the President was about to walk off the field, I made my move and headed to the backstop screen where "W" was patiently waiting. "Mr. President," I lightly shouted with a fist bump to the screen, and soon enough the 43rd President of the United States responded with a fist bump of his own. Standing eye to eye, albeit through a screen, fist bumping a former United States President was one precious moment I'd never imagine happening on August 21st at the MLB Classic game in Williamsport, Pennsylvania. I quickly said goodbye to the President, and with a broad grin on my face walked back to my seat near Mark and Randy. If that wasn't thrilling enough, what would ensue a few minutes later became one of the greatest exchanges I'd ever encountered. While I was talking to

Mark, Randy, Uncle Marlin, and Uncle Chuck about the brief, but super impactful, exchange I had with President Bush, we noticed a commotion in the stands down the first base line. It was George "W" flanked by secret service agents walking the concourse in between the lower and upper levels saying hello to energized fans of all ages.

As he walked towards our section, President Bush not only waved to the crowd, engaged in small talk with many, but also was courteous enough to stop for pictures for the fortunate at hand. Getting even closer to our section, I looked at Mark and said, "Let's go meet the Pres!" With much eagerness and beaming with smiles, we climbed the steps to the top of the concourse level and stood shoulder to shoulder waiting with open arms to potentially talk to one of the most iconic Presidents of our generation. President Bush was just a few feet away from his next stop, one of the Utah coaches. As their conversation was ending, I began to get a little anxious since that coach was standing in the way between me and Mark and President George W. Bush. The moment had come, President Bush had arrived, and with secret service agents surrounding him and snipers on the top of the stadium roof, I enthusiastically said, "Hello, Mr. President." Although I had just fist bumped him 10 minutes ago, he certainly didn't remember the priceless moment... and that was surely all right. With my right hand out, President Bush grasped my hand, and one of my most memorable handshakes occurred. For the next 20 seconds, I didn't let go, as I just kept shaking President Bush's hand. At one point, I thought one of the secret service agents was going to break up our handshake exchange. After shaking my hand, Mark got a firm shake in as well, and the President asked where we were from. I clearly stated we were from the great state of Tennessee and said that the Volunteer State loves President Bush. Before the President could move on to his next round of fans, I asked for a quick selfie. The President, Mark and I quickly posed together as I snapped off a few quick selfies. After saying our goodbyes, Mark and I just looked at each other in awe as meeting the past commander-in-chief was totally surreal. To this day, I still say that not many people can say they fist bumped, gave a handshake, and took a selfie with a former President of the United States, except for maybe me.

One of my most priceless selfies of all time –
Me, President George W. Bush, and Mark Carter

The fun didn't stop there as a few minutes after our chat with President Bush, Uncle Marlin brought down one of his golf buddies to meet the three coaches. After hearing Uncle Marlin's voice say, "Boys, I have someone I want you to meet," I quickly turned around and saw Hall of Famer, Mike Mussina, standing tall in his light blue shirt and khaki pants. As if the night couldn't get any better, the five of us chitchatted with the Orioles and Yankees legendary pitcher. Soon after our conversation with the "Moose," we noticed ESPN journalist and Vanderbilt graduate, Buster Olney, standing near our section. Of course, Mark had to get Buster's attention, and following a quick shout to Buster, the two of them talked for a little while.

The game finally began and was action packed from the start. Sitting a few rows back from the field, it was amazing for the boys to see these MLB super stars so close-at-hand. The third base coach for the Orioles, Tony Mansolino, paid our boys a few visits in between innings. The former Vandy Boy, and friend of Mark Carter, handed the boys some official MLB pearls and gum throughout the game. It was such a cool gesture from Coach Mansolino and certainly caught the attention of some of the other Little Leaguers and coaches in attendance. Another really special guest paid a visit to the team in the middle innings of the game; an umpire, who called balls and strikes during one of our Southeast Regional games, made a visit to Williamsport and took part in the flyover during the opening day ceremonies. It was not only great to visit with this esteemed Air Force pilot again, but also even more memorable because he gave the team unique, one-of-a-kind Air Force patches to bring back home.

As the night went on, each LLWS team was introduced while game highlights played on the jumbo scoreboard. After a back-and-forth affair between both teams, the Orioles finally prevailed with a 5-3 victory over the Red Sox. For the boys from Nolensville, it was a special day filled with unimaginable moments, mingling with MLB super stars at Lamade Stadium and watching a night cap MLB game only a few rows from home plate. Despite our team not playing a game that day, August 21, 2022, will go down as one of the most treasured days for me that summer. I will never forget the smiles and laughter from our players while they talked and hammed it up with many of the Red Sox and Orioles players. It did not matter if these brothers were on the ball field together, in their dorm, or watching an MLB game in a small, one-of-a-kind baseball stadium – these 13 young men shared a common bond and friendship that would become unmatched. For me, personally, meeting one of the most influential presidents in my lifetime was a moment I will never forget.

The night was ending, and we strolled out of the ballpark while saying our goodbyes to our families who also had the pleasure of watching that thrilling game that night. While the boys' energy was high when we got back to the dorms, we knew the team needed to rest up as tomorrow was going to be our biggest challenge yet. A scrappy Great Lakes team from Hagerstown, Indiana, was our next opponent in the U.S. winners-bracket quarterfinal game.

Monday, August 22nd

It was Monday morning, game day, but the weather forecast was not looking so optimistic. After my normal early morning routine of going for a long walk, and the team heading to breakfast, the boys chilled and hung out the rest of the day until we had to head over to the indoor cages for our pre-game BP. Like any other game day, before we started our march towards the security gates leading out of the International Grove, we made sure the team had all their gear. It was not uncommon to see at least one of the boys sprint back to the dorm for a forgotten cleat or other piece of important equipment. The renowned team-walk down the steps leading to the concourse of Lamade Stadium never got old. The team really looked forward to walking as one, signing autographs, and, of course, getting their pictures taken with energized fans.

After another stellar round of pre-game batting practice, we were ready to make our way to the stadium. The kids' parents, siblings, families, and friends always made us feel so welcome when we took our short walk from the indoor cages up the short hill to the entrance of Lamade Stadium. Ingle Martin, father of Wright, always greeted us with high fives, encouragement, and, of course, some must-have bottles of Mountain Dew. For some of the boys, including myself and "Mountain" Drew, it was a customary tradition to sip on some Dew prior to the game. Unfortunately, Mother Nature hit again, and our quarterfinal game vs. Indiana was delayed.

During the weather delay, we had two notable people visit us in the third base dugout. None other than ESPN commentors, Kyle Peterson and Jessica Mendoza, made their way to our dugout to talk baseball, answer questions, and hang out with the boys. Although the boys had a lot of fun with both Kyle and Jessica, I honestly think Randy, Mark, and I appreciated their company even more. The rain was not letting up, and Little League officials instructed us to once again head to the media room where we would lounge around until we received the all-clear to head back to the field.

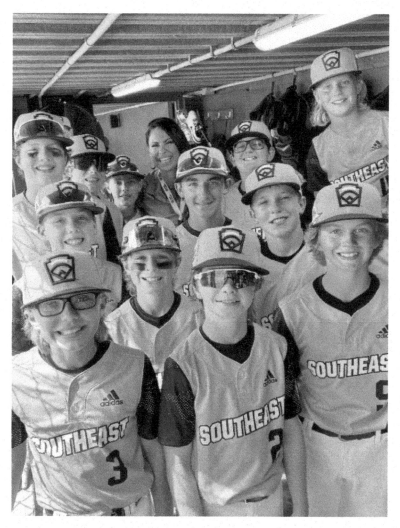

The boys and ESPN's Jessica Mendoza

It was routine for the boys while waiting through these rain delays to always take care of the Little League facilities. With their cleats full of mud, they would always take them off before entering the carpeted media room. As the weather delay went on, so did the shenanigans. To pass time, the coaches would often ask the boys trivia questions or further their education by having one-off spelling bees. We even had a few of the boys practice their post-game presser speeches. However, this rain delay was lingering, and the team was becoming hungry. It was time for a GroupMe message asking our parents for some food for these thirteen hungry young men. Within 15 minutes, Ben May and a few other parents knocked on the back door leading into the media interview room and delivered chicken tenders and pizza. With bellies full and even more energy to spare, the two-hour rain delay came to an end, and Little League officials gave us the green light to head back to the field for a condensed warm-up session before the start of the first pitch.

On the mound for Hagerstown Little League, representing the Great Lakes region, was their flame-throwing ace. We coaches had done some scouting days prior and knew this young ace was a fierce competitor who threw extremely hard. With the sun trying to make its way out, and the temperature around 75 degrees, the top of the first brought William Satinoff to the plate for the Southeast. On a 3-2 count, Sati lined a 72 MPH fastball to right field. After Satinoff led off with a base knock, Indiana's ace came back with three consecutive punchouts to end the top of the first inning. With four days' rest, we decided to bring back T-Rex to toe the rubber for this crucial semi-final winners bracket matchup. At the start, Trent got into a little jam giving up a walk followed by a hard-hit single to left field. With two men on, and no outs, Trent induced a weak ground ball that Sati corralled, fired a strike to Nash, and got the 6-4 force for the first out of the inning. Now with runners on first and third, the next Indiana batter laid down a perfectly placed safety squeeze. Like a cat, Trent hopped off the mound, gathered the ball, and threw a strike to first for the out, but the runner on third crossed the plate for the Great Lakes first run of the game. T-Rex gassed up the next batter for a swing and a miss ending the bottom of the first inning.

The top of the second inning was not much different from the previous inning for the Southeast. After back-to-back K's, Josiah Porter battled his way to a 3-2 count, only to be hit in the hip by a 70+ MPH heater. Tough as nails, Jo-Jo never rubbed it, gingerly trotted down to first base and was comforted by Coach Mark after he hit the bag. After Josiah walked it off and jogged back to first base, the Indiana ace greeted Josiah with a handshake and pat on the back followed by their second and third baseman coming over to check on Josiah as well. This occurrence was, indeed, another tremendous display of sportsmanship seen throughout the summer, this time Nolensville on the receiving end. Unfortunately, after Josiah made it to first, Indiana's pitcher kept delivering as he struck out his sixth batter of the game to end the top of the second inning. After back-to-back K's by McNiel, he got the third batter of the bottom of the second inning to pop up to Carter at second for the final out. It was 1-0, Great Lakes on top after two innings, and the pitching so far for both teams certainly did not disappoint.

After two consecutive outs in the top of the third, Rhodes scurried to second after Indiana's second baseman muffed a flare to short right field. Unfortunately, we had another runner left in scoring position as our eighth strikeout of the game ended the top of the third inning. Changing up his arm angles, from over the top to side arm, McNiel kept the Indiana batters off balance as he produced another 1-2-3 inning in the bottom of the third.

The top of the fourth inning brought a much-needed baserunner to start the inning off as Wright Martin reached on an error with a hot shot to shortstop that went through the wickets. On a 1-1 count, the next batter, Drew Chadwick, hit a towering fly ball over the head of the centerfielder. Not knowing if the centerfielder was going to catch the ball, Wright stopped at second base and the Southeast had a little rally cooking in the top of the fourth. With runners on first and second, and none out, up stepped Caz Logue, pinch hitting for Carter. Despite bunting not being one of this team's strengths, I had the utmost confidence in Caz and gave him the sacrifice bunt sign. As the smooth hitting lefty squared around, Indiana's pitcher threw a wild pitch advancing Wright to third and Drew to second. After a borderline strike three call to Caz, and a 74 MPH heater that rung up Josiah for the second out, up stepped T-Rex in a crucial two out situation. On a 1-2 count and his 75th pitch of the game, Indiana's ace uncorked a high wild pitch, scoring Martin with the tying run. With a few lucky breaks, we were able to scrap and claw and put a run on the board in the top of the fourth inning. With all the confidence in the world, and his pitch count remaining low, Trent strutted out to the mound in the bottom of the fourth inning. After getting the first batter on a ground out, the Great Lakes' next batter laced a line drive to right field and eventually made it to second after an errant pickup throw from Bo landed in right field. Cool as a cucumber, T-Rex responded with his fifth and sixth strikeouts of the game ending Indiana's threat in the bottom of the fourth inning.

With only a few more pitches to go until Indiana's ace hit his pitch limit, Lane Dever pinch hit for Grayson May and scorched a line drive to right for the first out. On a 2-2 count, Satinoff continued his hot streak vs. their ace as he stroked another single to right field. Fortunately for us, that was their superstar's last pitch as he exceeded the Little League pitch count. After two wild pitches from Indiana's lefty reliever, and a punchout to Jack Rhodes, Satinoff advanced all the way to third base. Then, with two outs, Bo Daniel hit a clutch, towering fly ball that hooked right inside the foul line for an RBI double scoring William for the go ahead run. It was now 2-1 Southeast, and out came T-Rex in the bottom of the fifth inning to toe the rubber. After another 6-3 assist from Satinoff, Trent McNiel bore down and recorded his impressive seventh and eighth punchouts of the game.

In the top of the sixth inning, Indiana's soft-tossing lefty began the inning with a strikeout. With one out, Charlie Malom stepped into the box pinch hitting for Chadwick and legged out an infield single for his first LLWS hit. Up next, pinch hitting for Caz Logue, was JF Forni who battled his way on with a walk. It was now first and second, and Josiah Porter followed with a four pitch walk to load the bases. After Trent lined out to center trying to help his own cause, Indiana's shortstop made a circus catch on Lane's floater to end the top of the sixth inning. Trent, who had thrown a gem of a game so far, headed out to the mound in the bottom of the sixth inning trying to finish what he started. We knew the bottom of the sixth would not be a layup as Indiana's top of the order was coming up. On the first pitch, their leadoff batter hit a hard ground ball that scooted past Wright at first. With Trent's pitch count rising and arguably the Great Lakes' best hitter coming up, Randy decided to make the call and bring in our stopper, Jack Rhodes. Next, on a 1-0 count, Indiana's slugger hit a rocket over Josiah's head in left that one hopped the fence and advanced the tying runner to third as he walked into second for a standup double. Setting up a force out to any base, the next Indiana batter was intentionally walked loading up the bases. It was now a 2-1 game in the bottom of the sixth inning with Tennessee on top, and the bases were loaded for Indiana with none out. Talk about being in a major jam with our backs against the wall. Miraculously, not one of our players, nor any of our coaches, panicked or showed any sign of giving up as this team was known for their resiliency, confidence, and grit throughout the entire summer. On a 3-2 count, the next Indiana batter laced a liner up the middle that hit off the mound and ricocheted into centerfield. The tying run crossed the plate, but Grayson May fielded the hard-hit ball cleanly, crow hopped, and made a perfect throw to Bo at the plate, holding off the potential game winning run. The Indiana bench erupted; their fans went crazy, and the stands flooded with yellow and black behind the third base dugout were quieted in disbelief.

If there was ever a time for the wily two veterans from Nolensville, Jack and William, to step up their game, it was right now. Step up they did as these two peak performers put the rest of their team on their backs and delivered what would be one of the best clutch performances in the 2022 Little League World Series. Now, still with none out, and the bases loaded in a 2-2 game, Jack had to face Indiana's number five, six and seven batters. With a 2-2 count, Jack reared back and pumped a fastball right by the Indiana batter for the first out of the inning. The next batter went down swinging, as well, chasing high cheese from none other, Jack & Cheese, for the second out of the inning. The suspense was high; many of the 6,498 fans were now on their feet, especially those passionate Indiana fans who presumably thought this game was in the books a few batters ago. Rhodes, up 0-2 on the count, threw a low outside fastball to the left-handed batter who hit a floating line drive to the hole between shortstop and third base. Out of nowhere, with a cape on his back, William Satinoff laid out to his backhand side, making one of the most incredible clutch plays in recent memory for the third out of the inning. It was another web-gem from Sati, keeping Tennessee alive as we headed to extra innings. One of my favorite candid shots of the summer came after that last diving play when Jack came up to William right after that catch and the two embraced each other with a vigorous hug.

It was now a whole new ball game and the momentum had now shifted back to Tennessee. As if it couldn't get any better, the top of the seventh inning was starting off with our number one, two, and three batters – Satinoff, Rhodes, and Daniel. Boom, on a 1-1 count, Sati hit a sharp ground ball to short, which the Indiana shortstop then fired across the diamond only to have the ball sail over the first baseman's head, landing out of play and advancing William to second base. Rhodes stepped to the plate next, and on a 0-1 count, crushed a hanging breaking ball past the second baseman to right field. On the crack of the bat, William put his head down, sprinted around third only to see my hand waving him in for the go ahead run. Sliding across the plate was William who, then, emphatically, pounded his chest and waved his hands up to the raucous Tennessee fans. Jack, who once again stepped up and delivered a monumental, clutch performance took second on the throw and clenched his hands together while looking into our dugout. The "Black - Gold" chant erupted from our side of the stadium as the flood gates were about to open. Bo Daniel, who had earlier in the game delivered an RBI double, came up big again as he hooked another long fly ball down the left field line, legging his way to third for an RBI triple, scoring Rhodes. After a popup out to first base by Wright, Drew Chadwick executed perfect situational hitting as he grounded out to the second baseman, scoring Daniel from third. It was now 5-2 Tennessee, and Indiana brought in another relief pitcher to try to end the damage. After a scorching, line-drive single to centerfield by Caz Logue, the inning ended, but not after three big runs were put on the board by this relentless team from Nolensville. The bottom of the seventh brought Jack back to the bump as we leaned on him to finish the game. In flawless fashion, Rhodes delivered a one, two, three inning propelling Tennessee to an extra-inning, thrilling defeat over a feisty Indiana ball club.

It was a total team effort to pull off this unthinkable win. We pounded out eight hits, scored five runs, and delivered some key situational hits. One that always comes to mind is Drew Chadwick's soft ground ball out to second in the top of the seventh inning. Drew's productive execution of situational hitting scored our fifth run of the game and showed that even an out can deliver success. Our pitchers were consistently around the plate giving our defense a chance as 64% of their pitches were thrown for strikes. There were so many clutch performances in this U.S. winners-bracket quarter final game. With, arguably, his best overall pitching performance of the series, T-Rex dominated the hitters of Indiana keeping them off balance with his array of pitches and deliveries, ultimately giving up only one earned run in five innings while striking out eight batters and walking only one.

Bo Daniel had a huge offensive game going 2-4 with a clutch RBI double and RBI triple. What can I say about the two savvy veterans, Satinoff and Rhodes? Some will call it clutch, others may point to their previous experience at the LLWS; however, I think it was their self-confidence, leadership, and ability to seize the moment that these two young men demonstrated in the defeat over Indiana. Jack came up huge with the game winning RBI single and displayed pitching mastery to get us out of a bases loaded no-out jam to force extra frames. William, with his countless ways of getting on base and being that sparkplug on offense, ultimately, saved the game with a Sportscenter web-gem in the bottom of the sixth inning. The victory vs. Indiana, in my opinion, will go down as one of the most thrilling games in recent memory. We Believe.

After the electrifying defeat over Indiana, Randy, William, and Trent headed to the media interview room. Typically, it was only the manager and select players that made their way to the post-game presser. I had asked Randy after the game if he would mind if I tagged along for this one. I was fortunate enough to sit in the room and take in the sights and sounds of these two amazing players and one heck of a manager talk about the big win vs. Indiana. Not surprisingly, one of the first questions asked was about William's catch in the bottom of the sixth inning. Speaking humbly, William said, "That was really cool just to get that catch and save the game." Trent was then asked how confident the team was, after getting out of that jam, that they were going to score runs in the top of the seventh inning. That word, confidence, appeared again as Trent talked to the reporters about how the momentum changed really fast, and he knew we were going to win after that half inning. Trent went on to talk about his pitching performance and how he caught the final out at first base. Furthermore, Trent, emotionally, talked about how no matter a person's size or how one looks, anyone can play this great game of baseball by just trying one's best. One of the reporters then asked both boys about Indiana's ace and the team's strategy against him. Trent mentioned how good the Indiana pitcher's two-seam fastball was, so he knew how to work the count, do his job, and do what's best for the team when he was at bat. Then, William said, "Kinda what he said. I tried to work the count, get him out as fast as possible, and get a new pitcher, and hit that dude." Following William's philosophical response, Randy, grinning, kiddingly said, "That was our game strategy; hit that dude." Being live in the press room, seeing the expressions on their faces, and hearing what they had to say about the game was so priceless. Randy further explained to the reporters that our goal was to get five to six pitch AB's and how that equated to getting a single. Eventually, the team would get to the starter, and because of pitch counts, we would see their bullpen. Randy was then asked about Jack's clutch performance on the mound. Most forget, but that game vs. Indiana was Jack's first appearance since the regional. Because he was dealing with some shoulder discomfort from where he was hit by a pitch in the regional, we had held him out until that Indiana game. Randy spoke about his mound visit in the bottom of the sixth and how he told all the boys about the confidence we all had in each other. Lastly, one of the reporters highlighted the fact that due to this win we'd be guaranteed a top three finish in the U.S. One of my favorite lines came from Trent, followed by Randy, as Trent said, "Knowing we are a top three team in the U.S. is crazy. The feeling that we've come a long way from the start. At the beginning we could barely catch a ball in the infield, but we battled. It's been a journey." Randy, smiling broadly, shrugged his shoulders, followed up, and said, "It's been a great journey; what a great summer." I couldn't have said it better myself, and that journey was about to get tested further as the boys from Hawaii were awaiting us in the U.S. winners bracket semi-final game slated for Wednesday, August 24th.

After the big win over Indiana, our players and coaches had the opportunity to spend some pleasant time with their families; many went out to dinner around downtown Williamsport. Fortunately, we had another day off to rest our arms, but taking a solid round of batting practice was still in the cards.

The next morning while walking towards my routine walking trail, I bumped into a Pennsylvania state policeman at the security gate. With his K-9 partner, a slender, brown and tan Belgian Malinois named Rom, the two law enforcement officers inspected various service vehicles that were scheduled to drop off items at the concession stands and beyond. In my typical dog-loving fashion, I had to stop and ask if I could say hello and greet the beautiful canine. As the state policeman and I chatted, I, of course, asked what he was feeding his dog. He fed Eukanuba in years past, but, unfortunately, now was feeding a competitor of Mars Petcare. Despite our differences about pet food, we continued to have a great conversation about his law enforcement career, dog food nutrition, and even talked about my brief law enforcement stint. After our back and forth, 15-minute conversation, I asked if I could get a quick picture with his partner. As I walked over to his patrol car, I greeted the young pup, put my hand around his head and got a terrific photograph with one of Pennsylvania's finest.

The rest of the day was spent relaxing, playing in the game room, and holding a productive round of BP. We knew a good night's sleep was needed since the biggest game of the summer was taking place the next afternoon.

Wednesday, August 24th

It was game day, and all eyes were on the 3:00 p.m. EST game. The talk around the International Grove was our matchup with the boys from the big island. The buzz around social media, other outlets, and Little League gurus was that it would be a David vs. Goliath type of game. The West region, represented by Honolulu Little League, had won three previous games leading into our U.S. winners bracket semi-final game. This powerhouse of a team had outscored their opponents 29-1, while out hitting the opposition 26-1. Their nasty staff of aces hurled two shutouts, including a no hitter against a tough, resilient New York team out of the Metro region. This well-oiled machine was oozing with confidence, ready to face another team on a hot streak of its own: the apparent gigantic underdogs, Nolensville Little League, proudly representing the Southeast region. After Randy, Mark, and I watched back games of this overpowering offense from Hawaii, we thought none other than Nash Carter with his filthy off-speed arsenal and ability to hit his spots would give us the best chance to slow down the explosiveness of Hawaii's bats.

It was a warm, 85-degree day with rays of sunshine beaming over iconic Lamade Stadium for Game #30 of the Little League World Series. Being the visiting team, we had the opportunity to strike first, but, unfortunately, Hawaii's southpaw induced a quick 1-2-3 inning retiring the side in order. The mighty 4'10" and 85 lbs. of Nash Carter took the mound in the bottom of the first inning for the Southeast. On the second pitch of the bottom of the first, Hawaii's leadoff man hit a low, Carter breaking ball to right centerfield that cleared the fence. It was already the third homerun of the LLWS for Hawaii's leadoff man, who, ironically, also played in the 2021 LLWS for Hawaii. After striking out the next batter, Nash got himself into a little jam, and with the bases loaded, the next Hawaii batter smashed a grand slam homerun making it a quick 5-0 lead in the bottom of the first inning. We had known this Hawaii team could hit, but little did we expect the barrage of power right from the start. After a walk and another base hit, Randy slowly walked to the mound to make a pitching change, and Nash changed spots with William at shortstop. Fortunately, Sati was able to help Nash out and get back-to-back outs ending the bottom of the first inning. It had been a long time since our team faced such a deficit, especially right out of the gate.

Wright Martin led off the top of the second inning with a scorcher to left field. With one out, and a man on first base, Nash hit a looping liner that hit off the pitcher's mitt making it first and second with one out. We had a bit of a rally going, and coming off the last half inning, this momentum certainly was encouraging. Unfortunately, Hawaii's lefty bore down, struck out Josiah, and induced a fly ball from Caz for the third out of the inning. Two left, no runs, and now Satinoff and the defense were heading back to the field to face Hawaii's meat of the order. After getting the leadoff hitter on a line drive out to May in center, their next batter hit a blooping double that fell between Porter and Logue. Then on a 2-0 count, Hawaii's cleanup hitter belted another long ball that hit off the Howard J. Lamade statue in centerfield for the team's third homerun of the game. As the ball left the bat, all one saw was William turning around, looking in disbelief, as Grayson jumped over the padded fence trying to rob the mammoth blast. It was déjà vu two batters later when the fourth homerun of the game was lifted into orbit for Hawaii's eighth run of the game. Finally, the inning ended, but not after another three runs crossed the plate.

Heading into the top of the third inning, and down by eight, we needed to put together a string of base knocks and get a rally started. The top of the third started off strong with a hit-by-pitch to Grayson May followed by a four-pitch walk to Satinoff. Similar to the last inning, two baserunners had gotten on base early in the inning. With a new arm on the mound for Hawaii, Jack came up with runners on first and second, none out, and hit a two hopper to the second base-men for a 4-6-3 twin killing. After a pop-up third out by Bo, Tennessee came away with a goose egg in the top of the third inning. After two quicks outs in the bottom of the third inning, Hawaii struck again as another round tripper was launched over the outstretched glove of May for Hawaii's ninth run of the game. For the hitters of Hawaii, it looked like beach balls were being tossed over the plate as five homeruns had already left the yard, and it was only the bottom of the third inning. Finally, after two consecutive base knocks and a walk, William was pulled from the mound. The pitching carousel had now begun as Bo Daniel took the mound to relieve William. With the bases loaded, Bo uncorked a wild pitch leading to Hawaii's 10th run of the game. After another walk, Randy walked to the mound and called upon our nasty knuckler, Wright Martin. Although Wright had not pitched much throughout the year, we knew the big righty was capable of slowing down this hitting machine. On a 2-0 count, the Hawaii hitter got jammed and punched a looping fly ball in front of Grayson in center scoring two more runs. As if the game could not get any worse, on that same play, the back swing of the batter caught Jack in the wrist immediately sending our backstop to the ground, wincing in pain. Unfortunately, Jack couldn't continue, left the field, and was immediately evaluated by the Little League training staff. Down 12, and now our leader and one of our most dominant hitters in the tournament was out of the game due to an injury. Obviously, the game went on, but all our thoughts were on Jack, not knowing the severity of his wrist injury. There were now two outs, with runners on first and third, and a sharp line drive was scorched under the diving glove of Satinoff for the 13th run of the game. Wright finished the bottom of the third inning with a swinging strikeout for his first "K" of the game.

We were heading to the top of the fourth inning, and due to the 10-run rule, we needed some offense to keep the game going. Unfortunately, the fourth inning was no different from the previous three, as we went down in quick fashion with 1-2-3 consecutive outs. Ball game. In front of a crowd of 12,007, Hawaii put on another dominant performance and punched their way into the United States Championship game. Like the rest of the teams that faced Hawaii previously, we were no test for this juggernaut of a team. Having given up 13 runs, 12 hits, and producing a measly two hits on offense, this Tennessee team could have easily put their heads down and thrown in the towel. However, never once did we coaches, our parents, or the Nolensville Little League fans across the nation ever think that would occur. Resiliency and confidence were two underlying words that had consistently described this team of 13 brothers. The humiliating defeat by Hawaii certainly stung, but knowing the LLWS was a double-elimination tournament gave us less than 24 hours to shake off the dirt, move forward, and regroup as united as ever.

In the night cap, a strong Texas team, representing the Southwest, defeated Pennsylvania out of the Mid-Atlantic region, setting up an elimination game the next day between Texas and Tennessee. All eyes would be tuned in for this heavyweight matchup with the winner advancing to the United States Championship game on Saturday, August 27th vs. Hawaii on ABC. We Believe.

Thursday, August 25th

After a good night's sleep, putting yesterday's rough showing against Hawaii behind us, the boys felt rejuvenated and as confident as ever to take on Pearland Little League, representing Texas and the Southwest, later that night. Some of the best news of the week came when we were told Jack was cleared to play vs. Texas. It was a huge relief to say the least as we knew we would need our veteran catcher in the lineup vs. Texas.

I woke up early that morning, and since a bit of superstition had been part of this journey to date, I decided to change up my early morning routine after the big-time loss. Before heading for my usual walk in the park, I headed to Volunteer Stadium. With my AirPods in, and Spotify listings blaring, I jogged from one end of the bleachers to the other, taking each step one by one.

Finally, our pre-game batting practice was closing in, and our team was ready to make another walk from the International Grove down the steep steps leading to Lamade Stadium's concourse. There was an international elimination semi-final game being played at Lamade that afternoon between Mexico and the

Caribbean. Throughout the LLWS, the international teams had played at Volunteer Stadium, but since the field of 20 was down to the top eight teams in the world, all games moving forward were played at the legendary Lamade Stadium.

As our team made its way through the concourse of the stadium heading to the indoor batting cages, the fanfare grew larger. By now the boys were used to being stopped for pictures, and autographs, but tonight's game was even more hyped due to what was at stake. Following a loose, but focused, round of pre-game batting practice, we started to make our walk from the indoor cages to the entrance of Lamade Stadium behind home plate. I remember Mark sending a GroupMe message to the parents asking if someone could bring the boys some pizza and chicken tenders as stomachs were churning with much anticipated excitement and hunger as well.

Drew Chadwick signing autographs for two of Nolensville's biggest fans, JB & Caleb

We were the home team and in the first base dugout for the #34 game of the 2022 LLWS. It was a warm, 80-degree night with the stands a sea of yellow and black representing the Volunteer State and orange and yellow embodying the Lone Star State. On the mound for Tennessee was a kid that we had called on before in big game situations, none other than righty, Drew Chadwick. Whether it was closing the door against Goodlettsville in the district finals or throwing an absolute gem vs. Virginia to punch our ticket to Williamsport, Drew was the pitcher we wanted on the mound to take on a powerhouse team from Texas that had just won two straight games and was riding a high going into this United States semi-final elimination game.

The first pitch was 7:10 p.m., and the top of the order for Texas brought up their shortstop, arguably, one of the best players in the tournament. On a 2-2 count, their leadoff batter laced an opposite field, stand-up double to open the game. The next batter hit a shallow fly ball that dropped just in front of Grayson May, scoring Texas's first run of the game. Coming off an absolute run-ruled thrashing by Hawaii the night before, and now back-to-back hits leading to the first run of the game for Texas, Drew Chadwick could have become flustered in disbelief and, potentially, shut down. However, Drew, who had been known for wearing his emotions on his sleeve, took a deep breath, settled in, and pitched what would be his most dominant performance of the year. With a runner now on first base, the next batter hit a hard ground ball to William at short. Stepping to his right, he backhanded the hot shot, threw a strike to Nash at second base, who made a lightning quick turn at second for a 6-4-3 double play. After Chadwick produced the pitcher's best friend, a seeing-eye single eluded the outstretched lunges of Wright and Nash and trickled into right field for Texas's third hit of the inning. Following the base hit, Drew came back with high heat striking out the final batter of the inning.

The bottom of the first started off with a called third strike to Sati, followed up by Jack's eighth hit of the LLWS, a single to right field. Bo-Bo followed up with a screamer of a line drive right back up the box that ricocheted off the pitcher's glove for an infield base hit. On a 0-2 count, Wright delivered with a great piece of hitting by staying back on a hanging breaking ball and sending a line drive to center field. After Drew went down swinging on a nasty off-speed pitch, up came Josiah Porter with two outs and three ducks on the pond. Jo-Jo, who had come up clutch in big game situations throughout the post-season, produced an energy that thundered 785 miles back home in Nolensville. On a 2-1 count, with the bases juiced, Porter crushed a belt-high fastball over the centerfield fence for a grand slam. "Holy Cow," just like that, after going down 1-0 in the top of the first inning, we got a wake-up call, put together a string of base hits, and delivered on what would become one of the most electrifying and memorable dingers I'd ever witnessed. As Josiah rounded first, he looked back at our dugout, clapped his hands, and raised them up with pure jubilation. I'll never forget the radiant smile on Josiah's face while rounding third when I had my right hand opened wide for our customary "Big Hand Joe" handshake. As Josiah stomped his powerful right foot on home plate, his ecstatic teammates mobbed him with hugs and extra-loving knocks to the helmet, congratulating him on the biggest hit of his young career. After the Vandy Boys-like stomp on home plate, Josiah hopped back to the dugout with his hands up in the air shouting, "Let's Go," to our Tennessee fans that were on their feet rejoicing in pure delight. Josiah, an inspiration on and off the diamond, had beat so many odds. Blind in his right eye from a childhood accident, he once again showed the world stage that nothing could hold him back. Now, with the crowd back in their seats, Nash stepped up and hit a shallow fly ball to left field, only to be robbed by Texas's left fielder for the third out. After one, it was 4-1, Tennessee on top, and due to Josiah's clutch round trip, the momentum had everlastingly turned in favor of the boys in yellow and black.

Drewbie jogged out in the top of the second with a three-run lead behind him and a defense poised to back him up. Despite the epic bottom of the first inning, our team took nothing for granted, and knew this Texas ballclub was extremely talented up and down their lineup. After a man reached on an error, and a ground ball base hit to left field, Chadwick faced Texas's toughest out in the lineup with runners on first and second and two out. One slight mistake, and it could have been a brand-new game, but leaning on his sharp Uncle Charlie, Chadwick induced a towering fly ball to right field that was caught by Porter right on the warning track for the third out of the inning. The hits just kept on coming in the bottom of the second. Sweet swinging, Caz Logue, started off the inning with a hard-hit line drive to centerfield. Unfortunately, after Caz's hit, we couldn't get anything going as William ended the inning, hitting into a 6-4-3 double play.

Drew started the top of the third inning on fire, setting down their number two batter looking for his third strikeout of the game. With one out, Texas's next batter hit a ground ball deep in the hole to Sati. Running full speed to his backhand side, William fielded the ball, and in the same motion with a lightning-quick release, threw, off balance, a one-hop bullet to a stretched-out Wright Martin at first. A bang-bang play, the umpire, initially, called the runner safe. I vividly remember walking towards Randy in the dugout after the call saying, "You need to challenge this one." Challenge he did, and after the umpire put the headsets on to review the call, it was, eventually, overturned for the second out of the inning, adding another elite defensive play to William's resume. Drew just kept throwing strikes, and more ground ball outs ensued with Caz at third base making the final out of the third inning. The bats were silenced in the bottom of the third inning as Tennessee went down 1-2-3 to end the third.

Chadwick kept rolling in the top of the fourth. After a batter reached base with an infield single, Drew came back strong producing a fly ball out to Josiah in left and a long fly ball out to right centerfield, beautifully tracked down by Mullet Man, Grayson May, for the third out of the inning. Drew continued to dominate the heavy hitters from Texas, and with his exceptional defense backing him up, our confidence was growing inning by inning. Helping his own cause in the bottom of the fourth inning, Chadwick got on with a hit-by-pitch. Josiah followed up with a chopper to third base and, initially, was called out. Randy, on a roll with his manager challenges, decided to dispute this call as well, and, fortunately, won another one. A hit-by- pitch, followed up by a hustling infield hit, Tennessee was looking to add to its lead with some insurance runs. After a Texas pitching change, up stepped Charlie Malom, pinch hitting for Nash, and looking to deliver a clutch base hit. Unfortunately, Charlie struck out looking, but not before Drew and Josiah advanced to second and third on a wild pitch. With one out, JF Forni came up to the plate, pinch hitting for Caz. Forni, known for his grittiness and ability to grind out AB's, came up with a bigtime base knock as he scorched a 1-0 fastball to centerfield, scoring Chadwick with our fifth run of the game. Wow, talk about someone coming off our bench and stepping up in a pressure-packed moment, JF did just that. T-Rex was up next with runners on first and third looking to break this game wide open. On the first pitch, Trent hit a lined shot over the pitcher's head. As the second baseman scooted to the ball, he amazingly grabbed it with his barehand, stepped on second base and threw a short hop to first which was nicely dug out by the first baseman for an impressive unassisted double play to end the bottom of the fourth inning.

Up 5-1 heading into the top of the fifth, Chadwick continued to paint the black and set down Texas bats as another 1-2-3 inning occurred. The bottom of the fifth started off slowly with two consecutive outs. In the dugout, Randy called over Lane Dever and told him he was pinch hitting for Bo Daniel. Lane said, "Coach, do you want me to drop down a bunt?" "Absolutely not," Randy replied. "I want you to hit a double down the line, and when you get to second base, I want you to flex your muscles." Sure enough, on the first pitch he saw, Lane-O ripped a double down the left field line for a stand-up two-bagger. When Lane rolled into second base with a smile that could only be described as beaming, he raised his right arm, pointed to his flexed almighty bicep, looked into the dugout, and yelled, "Coach!" What a call from Randy, and an even better performance by Lane with some two-out bingo to continue the bottom of the fifth inning. Wright kept the inning alive by keeping his swing short and delivering another solid line drive to centerfield, scoring Dever with the sixth run of the game. Chadwick followed Martin with a little blooper over the head of the third baseman advancing Wright to third. With runners on first and third, I decided to call the infamous "fall down" play. It was a hoax of a baserunning play that was pulled off brilliantly last year by Jack Rhodes in the Southeast Regional but, unfortunately, had not been successfully executed to date this post season. I quickly went through the signs at third, and after the first pitch to Josiah, Drew intentionally stumbled, fell, and caused a distraction on the base path making the catcher throw down to first. As Drew quickly got up, a pickle ensued, and Wright came sprinting home for our seventh run of the game. After the first baseman threw to second, a foot race followed, and Drew was finally tagged out but only after executing a flawless "fall down" play. It was super rewarding to see this play come to life and, successfully, executed since we had worked on it from our first day of practice earlier in the summer.

Drew, who was on pitch 70, trotted out in the top of the sixth looking to finish what he started. Despite a leadoff base hit, Drew was able to get the next batter to hit into a 4-6 force out for the first out of the inning. Another swinging strikeout for Chadwick led to the second out. Then, on a 1-2 count, Drew quickly pitched and threw an outside fastball that the batter chased for his sixth strikeout of the game and the final out. Clenching his arms together and yelling passionately into the air, Drew Chadwick strutted off that mound with absolute pride and joy as he had thrown a masterful one-run, complete game to lead our team to victory over a top-notch Texas ballclub.

Coming off a drubbing by Hawaii the day before, some thought this was the end of the road for the Southeast champions. However, this team certainly stepped up to the challenge, came together, and rebounded as a unified group to put up an all-around clutch performance vs. the Southwest. All facets of the game were executed with precision that night. Once again, Drew Chadwick was called upon for a must-win game and absolutely shone. One of the fiercest competitors I know, Mountain Drew took this challenge head on and pitched one heck of a game, giving up one run, six hits, no walks, and striking out six Texas batters. The defense came up big again, providing a stellar performance all around the diamond. The offense rebounded nicely pounding out 10 hits, many of which were clutch in nature. Wright Martin continued his consistent play at the plate with two hits, two runs scored, and an RBI. Josiah Porter went 2-2, hitting the magical grand salami that provided the spark this team so greatly needed in the bottom of the first inning.

After we shook hands with the Texas team, everyone except Randy, Drew, and Josiah headed back to the van to take us back to International Grove. One of my favorite all-time moments was watching the video Mark sent to the parents of the boys on the bus, following the huge victory against Texas, celebrating in Nolensville fashion: the boys, with smiles flashing, were shouting, "Hey, hey, hey,

hey," followed by Mark, giving his legendary imitation of "Nature Boy" Ric Flair's, "WOOOO." United States Championship game here we come! We Believe!

While we were headed back to International Grove following the amazing "W" against Texas, Randy and the two stars of the game, Drew and Josiah, made their way to the media room for the post-game press conference. Not surprisingly, the first question for Josiah was how he felt after blasting his first inning grand slam. Modestly, with a stoic voice, Josiah said, "It felt amazing; I looked up at my dad. He was so happy. It's so good to put a smile on his face. It also put a smile on mine and everyone watching back home. I knew it was a great thing to do, and we got the win." A true representation of selflessness, despite it being the biggest hit ever for Nolensville Little League and of Josiah Porter's career, he reflected on his dad's reaction and what his hit did for the Tennessee fans. The reporter then asked him about what it was like in the dugout and how the team reacted following the "shot heard round the world." Jo-Jo said, "It got the energy up in the dugout; everyone knew that we could win this game. We just got to get a few runs and keep on believing." Drew was then asked how confident he felt having that 4-1 lead after the grand slam. Drew replied, "After that, I was just going crazy in my mind. I'm going to shut down this game. I mean, even if we don't score again, we are still going to win because I'm going to shut it down, and that's what I did." There it was again, the word confidence coming to light. Even though Drew did not say the actual word, his description of how he felt after that grand slam showed the volumes of confidence that he had in himself and his teammates who surrounded him on the diamond that night.

Then, Randy was asked about the pitching strategy and how we went with Drew for the must win game vs. Texas. Randy went on to say how confident we were with Drew and what he had done when he stepped in for Jack in the Southeast Regional championship vs. Virginia. Next, he explained how Jack's wrist had been injured by a Hawaii batter's backswing the day before. Continuing, Randy spoke about our strategy of starting Drew vs. Texas, noting that if trouble had arisen, Jack would have been the next man in line to pitch. Furthermore, that's why Jack was pulled from behind the plate and put in right field after the third inning; according to Little League rules, if a player catches four innings, that player can't pitch. Jokingly, Randy talked about the two challenges he won during the Texas game, and that they were his first challenges ever that he defeated. It was certainly a small victory for him, personally.

Randy was then asked about how the team came out and bounced back from a disappointing loss to Hawaii. Randy said, "That's just who this team is. They're gritty, you know, we don't have a lot of super stars on this team. We are a really good team, and if you look at the stat sheet, you see that every single time there's a different name at the top of it with somebody that did something special and that's what we pride ourselves in. So, we are gritty, we're resilient, and if someone can't get it done, there's always somebody there to jump up and get it done for us, and it seemed to work for us so far, and we'll see what happens." Randy also spoke about the rematch vs. Hawaii coming up and how the odds were against us but made it clear that Hawaii was beatable. He was then asked about how the moment felt, getting to the U.S. Championship game. Huth replied, "We are top two teams in the country right now, top four teams in the world. We never thought this would happen, you know. We believed in ourselves, but the chances of getting to this point are so hard. You have to have so many breaks, a little bit of luck, a whole lot of skill, and to get here is virtually impossible. You know, and after going 0-2 last year, to come back and do it this year for our community is just a magical experience. I'm sure everybody on our team would say the exact same thing is that Man, this is, what a ride."

A magical ride it was, and we were certainly not done as Nolensville had a rematch coming up with Hawaii. David vs. Goliath Part II was still awaiting us, and before that game would take place on championship Saturday, all of us were going to celebrate this momentous, life-changing win with our families that night. After the team dropped off their equipment at the dorms, we all scampered down to the bullpen area where a few tents were propped up for parents to meet with their players following games. That evening was super special as our boys spent invaluable moments with loved ones, reminiscing about what would be the tournament's biggest night to date, and again, in typical Nolensville fashion, the team was extremely hungry following the game. In for the save were Kelly and Maren, mothers of Lane and Jack, who made a quick McDonald's run for the boys. What made this night even more memorable were the two Pearland Texas Little Leaguers who hung out with our team following their defeat. Despite the big loss and their phenomenal team heading home the next day, their shortstop and left fielder befriended some of our players. That night wasn't about winning or losing, Texas vs. Tennessee; it was truly about a bunch of 11 and 12-year old's hanging out, living it up together at the Little League World Series. Still to this day, William and Jack keep in touch with Pearland's all-star shortstop as the bond they formed will, hopefully, stay true for years to come. After some well spent time with our families, and an extended curfew for our players, this most unforgettable night came to an end with Nolensville Little League heading to its first ever Little League World Series United States Championship game.

Friday, August 26th

Although the food accommodations during our stay in Williamsport were plentiful, our boys were always up for some morning treats. During our stay Mark made stops at a local McDonalds and brought back some of the boys' favorite breakfast menu items. The morning after the big Texas victory, Ingle Martin was nice enough to drop off assorted Dunkin Donuts, which the boys absolutely devoured.

Today was going to be a day for our players to spend worthy time with their families who had sacrificed so much throughout the summer. Our boys were ready to do so, and I know all our families were ready as well. All of us were on our own that Friday, and Randy made sure parents knew all the kids had to be back at the dorms by 9:30 p.m.

"Williamsport Welcomes the World," a customary festival held annually in downtown Williamsport, was taking place that Friday. The festival, which included many local merchants and food vendors, also had a very special guest signing autographs that day. Rickey Henderson, stolen base king and baseball Hall of Famer, made the trip down to Williamsport. Ironically, during my childhood, my favorite MLB player was non-other than Rickey himself. Needless to say, I was super excited to meet one of my childhood idols that day. I was also a bit jealous since T-Rex had met him earlier in the day and even got a selfie taken with the baseball legend. Many families had plans to attend the festival at some point during the day.

After my family and I stopped at a local mini-golf joint to get 18 holes in, we decided to venture downtown and walk the festival streets. The line to meet Rickey Henderson was fairly short, so the boys and I decided to jump in it and patiently wait our turn. When it was our turn, William, Jack, and I approached the table and, ecstatically, greeted the baseball icon. As he handed us a pre-signed autographed picture, I, animatedly, said, "Rickey, you were my favorite player growing up." Unfortunately, Rickey being Rickey continued to look down, signed his picture, and said absolutely not one word to me. Nevertheless, Henderson's rudeness and unwillingness to respond to my comment didn't faze me one bit. Really, it didn't because here I was at 47 years old, reveling in a once in a lifetime experience with our Nolensville Little League team about to play for the U.S. Championship game the next day, and nothing could take away from that.

After the "Williamsport Welcomes the World" festival, families went out to dinner, and many of us met up at a local ice cream parlor in the downtown area for some late-night sweets. As the 9:30 p.m. curfew approached, parents hustled their kids back to the front gate of International Grove. One by one, the boys and coaches badged in, went through the metal detector, and headed back to the dorm for a good night's sleep.

Saturday, August 27th

I woke up a little bit earlier Saturday morning with much anticipation and excitement for what was about to take place at 3:00 p.m. EST. As I headed for my morning exercise routine, I couldn't help but notice the long line of fans already in line on the side street leading up to the entrance of the Little League complex. When I crossed the street, I asked one of the security guards how long ago the line had been forming. The guard replied, "The line started forming in the early hours of the morning." This entire experience to date had been so surreal, but to see with my own eyes the fans lining up to see the team I helped coach, hours and hours before gametime, gave me absolute chills.

We had another big surprise for the boys that morning. James McCann, catcher for the New York Mets, and his wife Jess – Franklin, Tennessee, residents – sent a care package for the boys. The McCanns, two of the boys' biggest fans, had been following the team's success and wanted to give them a small token of appreciation for all their hard work. While the kids were getting dressed, the coaches laid out the array of gifts on a picnic table outside our dorm and covered them up so the boys had to wait with great anticipation to uncover their surprise. In true giving fashion, each player received a pair of Viper sunglasses, Stance socks, and a $100 gift card to Dick's Sporting Goods, all compliments of James and Jess McCann.

After breakfast, we headed down to Volunteer Stadium for another one of my favorite experiences this summer. It was 10:00 a.m., just five-plus hours before our U.S. Championship game, but all our attention was on the Little League Challenger Division's annual game between Mason (Ohio) Youth Organization Little League and Cambrian Park Little League (San Jose, California). Founded in 1989, The Little League Challenger Division is Little League's adaptive baseball program for individuals with physical and intellectual challenges. Today, there are over 950 Challenger programs in 10 countries around the world. For our own team host, Uncle Chuck, the Challenger Division is near and dear to his heart as he's been involved with the Challenger Division for the last 17 years. For the next hour, we met with the players and coaches of both teams, giving these extraordinary all-stars high fives, fist bumps, hugs, and words of encouragement. As we spent time with these two teams on the field prior to the first pitch, it was pretty emotional to look up in the stands and see their parents waving and shouting their kids' names while their eyes filled with tears of joy and appreciation. Randy was even able to get in a quick pitching lesson as he worked on mechanics with one of California's pitchers. For us three coaches, 13 players, Uncle Marlin, and Uncle Chuck, it was the least we could do that Saturday morning. To see all the smiles and excitement from those players from Ohio and California was certainly worth the price of admission.

After meeting with both teams, we headed into the stands to watch the annual challenger game. Before the game started, Jack Rhodes was lucky enough to catch the first pitch thrown out by none other than, yes, that guy, Rickey

Henderson. In Jack & Cheese style, after shaking Rickey's hand, he went on and, confidently, told him he would have thrown him out back in his playing days. This hilarious exchange from Jack still goes down as one of the best one-liners of the summer. The challenger game was truly all about these Little League all-stars from Ohio and California. Nobody kept score; everyone hit and was able to run the bases. Every player there was having such a blast with non-stop encouragement from their amazing volunteer coaches and coordinators.

After cheering on our new favorite teams from Ohio and California, we walked back to the International Grove with a true feeling of purpose. As we walked, I thought to myself that it will not just be the smiles, laughs, and positive energy displayed by these two teams or the emotional cheers of their proud parents that I will remember most, but, rather, it will be the inspiring acts of kindness that our boys showed these special youngsters and the abundance of happiness and gratification they, and we coaches, enjoyed in doing so.

After eating lunch, we headed over to the indoor cages for our pre-game batting practice. There was a different feeling of confidence from our boys that early afternoon. Despite getting ready to play in the biggest game of their young careers, there was a stoic, extra-loose kind of feeling before the game.

Following a very productive round of BP, we took our customary walk up the hill past Volunteer Stadium to the back section of Lamade Stadium where the Hawaii team was sitting patiently, watching the International Championship between Curacao and Chinese Taipei. We joined Hawaii and sat down to watch the conclusion of the International Championship game. What a great scene it was: the two U.S. finalists whose cities were 4,339 miles apart from each other – 26 Little Leaguers and six coaches about to compete in just under an hour – sitting side by side watching fellow Little League all-stars from Curacao and Chinese Taipei. As the International Championship wrapped up with a thrilling 1-0 Curacao victory, I couldn't help but notice the players from Chinese Taipei walking past us with tears of sadness, heading to their awaiting van to take them back to the Grove. Nonetheless, both Hawaii and Tennessee players and coaches demonstrated admirable sportsmanship by offering up high fives, congratulating the Curacao and Chinese Taipei teams for a game well played.

Finally, we made it to our third base dugout, and the boys began to stretch and throw before we took our phantom infield. Before the first pitch, Mark and I made sure we both got treasured pictures of us with our sons with the epic Lamade Stadium outfield in the background.

Father and son before the start of the U.S. Championship game

It was game time; with the starting lineups introduced, and traditional handshakes exchanged, Tennessee stood on the third base line with our hats off and our right hands over our hearts, proudly looking into centerfield where a giant American flag was being held for the singing of our national anthem. One of my favorite all-time pictures taken was of this exact moment – two amazing Little League teams from opposite sides of the country, standing on their respective first and third base lines, looking out to the American flag in centerfield with the illustrious Lamade green hills, filled shoulder to shoulder with a sea of fans.

Finally, on this sunny, 83-degree Saturday afternoon in Williamsport, Pennsylvania, Game #36 between Tennessee and Hawaii was about to begin. Our boys were pumped, confident as ever having put the previous loss vs. Hawaii behind them. Our parents, families, friends, and Tennessee fans who had taken this summer journey with us, step by step, were aglow in yellow and black behind the third base dugout and beyond. It was simply amazing to see so many fans aside from our parents and families repping our traditional black and yellow colors throughout the LLWS and especially during the U.S. Championship game. Our team from the start had a solid following from fans of all ages, but that day they came out stronger than ever. Our proud town of Nolensville, entire state of Tennessee, and fans across the globe were ready to tune in on ABC and cheer on this team of sensational young men. As the first pitch grew closer, I stepped outside the dugout before trotting to the third base coach's box and looked around to see 26,834 zealous Little League fans, truly a sight I'll never forget.

The top of the first ended up in a quick 1-2-3 as Satinoff, Rhodes, and Daniel were retired in order. On the mound for Tennessee was none other than T-Rex, Trent McNiel. The big righty was one of our most reliable pitchers throughout the summer, and all three coaches had the utmost belief in Trent in this U.S. Championship game. We knew going in that Trent would need to keep the dominant hitters from Hawaii off balance with his array of different arm angles and not be afraid to go after them. After two consecutive fly ball outs in the bottom of the first, Hawaii's number three-hole batter singled on a line drive to Bo in left field. Then on a 2-1 count their clean-up batter hit a line drive double over the head of Bo scoring Hawaii's first run of the game. The Hawaii fans dressed in their baby blue and yellow were on their feet as their team started off red hot like the last time we faced off. Trent, super composed and confident as ever, was able to induce a weak pop up to Sati at short for the third out of the inning. Well, compared to the last time we played this Hawaii squad coming, out of the first with only giving up one run was a big win in our book.

The top of the second inning started off in our favor with Wright reaching first base on catcher's interference. Then Drew and Josiah both punched out as Hawaii's ace was firing 73 MPH heaters while mixing in some nasty breaking balls. After Martin advanced on a wild pitch to second, Nash ended the inning with a roll over grounder to second base for the third out of the inning. Hawaii's bottom of the second inning started off with a line drive that bounced off the left field wall. Bo made a tremendous play by getting the ball in quickly to William, holding the Hawaii hitter to a long single. Playing some unexpected small ball, the next Hawaii hitter laid down a sacrifice bunt, only to have Trent bounce off the mound like a cat, field the ball cleanly, and hurl a strike to William at second for the force out. The next batter battled his way on with a full count walk and both runners advanced after a wild pitch. Now, with men on second and third for Hawaii, and one out, Hawaii demonstrated some successful situational hitting as their next batter hit a hard ground ball that was nicely fielded by Nash, scoring the runner from third. It was back to the top of their order and another run scored as their leadoff batter hit a nasty pitch by Trent right up the box for an RBI single. The bottom of the second inning ended as Nash caught a towering pop up for the third out of the inning.

Unfortunately, the top of the third was a quick inning as McNiel, May, and Satinoff went down in order 1-2-3. T-Rex trotted out for the bottom of the third and, boy, did he deliver a quick inning inducing a pop out, fly out, and ground ball out for a speedy bottom of the third inning. Three days prior when we played Hawaii, after three innings, it was 13-0 Hawaii on top, and our team was deflated to say the least. Today, in the biggest game of the year, we were totally in the game, only down by three heading into the top of the fourth inning.

Jack Rhodes led off the top of the fourth inning, and on a 1-2 count, hit an absolute rocket landing at the base of the right field fence for a long single. Up next was Bo Daniel, and, following a wild pitch, we now had a runner on second with nobody out and Tennessee threatening. Bo hit a towering pop up to the second baseman who drifted backwards and, uncharacteristically, dropped the ball advancing Rhodes to third. Wright Martin stepped up next with runners on first and third and no outs. Wright hit a check swing dribbler to the catcher who threw a laser to first base to beat Martin by a half step. It was a bang-bang play, and knowing our luck with replays throughout the series, Randy decided to contest this one as well. Unfortunately, the out call stood for the first out of the inning. It certainly wasn't Wright's hardest ball hit throughout the summer, but he did his job, put the ball in play, and delivered some good situational hitting to bring Jack home from third for our first run of the game. The Hawaii ace settled down after giving up his first run of the game, punching out Chadwick and Porter for his fifth and sixth K's of the game. Heading into the bottom of the fourth, we had put a run on the board cutting Hawaii's lead to two. The bottom of the fourth started off with a hit-by-pitch by Trent. Their next batter hit a high towering fly ball to centerfield causing Josiah to back track to the wall and jump in the air. Unfortunately, Josiah ran out of real estate, and the ball landed over the fence for a two-run bomb. Just like that, Hawaii responded to put another two runs on the board and now led 5-1. After giving up another single, and hit-by-pitch, T-Rex, ultimately, came back and struck out two more batters in the bottom of the fourth leaving two men stranded. Although we were down four heading into the top of the fifth, we still believed, and knew if we were to get some bingo going, we'd have a chance to scrap and claw for some runs in the last two innings of play.

Our Nolensville fans were always on their feet cheering us on –
U.S. Championship game

Caz Logue started off the top of the fifth and hit a hard-liner to shortstop for the first out. Trent, who battled his way to a 3-2 count, went down swinging on a 72 MPH fastball. Lane-O stepped to the plate with two outs, and on a 1-2 count delivered a line drive base hit to left field. With Hawaii's pitcher at the 85-pitch limit, they made a call to the bullpen and brought in their right fielder to relieve Hawaii's ace. On the first pitch, Satinoff hit a one hopper to shortstop for a 6-4 force out ending the top of the fifth inning. In the bottom of the fifth, Trent generated a pop up for the first out of the inning. Never afraid to work inside the entire game, Trent hit two more batters in the bottom of the fifth only to leave them stranded as the third out of the fifth inning was caught by Drew.

We were down to our last AB's, the top of the sixth inning, and our 2-3-4 batters were due up. Before Jack stepped up to the plate, Randy provided some words of inspiration and encouragement: "It's time to dig deep, ok, we got to get some base runners. We're not done yet. We're not done until the final out is made. Let's get some baserunners and see what happens. Let's put the pressure on them. Put the pressure on those guys. Hit the baseball and let's run around a little bit. Let's have a whole lot of fun, and let's win this game, and if we don't... who cares; let's have fun right now. Ok, we're here, we're here, we're here right now. We can do this. I believe in every single one of you. I know you believe, too. Let's go! Let's go!" Then, with the entire team huddled around Randy with their hands in tight, the shout of "We What? We Believe!" echoed throughout the third base dugout. Sweet Swinging Jack Rhodes continued his torrid hitting streak and tattooed another ball to centerfield for a leadoff single. With Jack on first, JF came to the plate and on a 1-1 count hit a dart of a line drive to second, only to have Jack doubled off for a double play. Down to our final out, up came Wright, but, unfortunately, the Hawaii pitcher won the battle striking out Wright for the final out of the game. It was over, but our boys from Nolensville never quit, competed until the very end, and put up a fight against the best team in the world. Coming into this U.S. Championship game, most everybody but our Tennessee faithful predicted Hawaii to steamroll over Tennessee similar to what had happened a few days prior. However, this resilient group of 13 Little Leaguers dug deep, played with confidence, and battled what could, arguably, be one of the best Little League World Series teams of all time.

The U.S. championship game averaged 2.41 million television viewers from around the world. Earlier in the week the MLB Little League Classic game received 1.18 million television viewers, and the Saturday prime time MLB game of the week on Fox, which included the Braves and Cardinals, averaged 1.94 million viewers. What a thrill it was to see the Little Leaguers outplay the big leaguers when it came to the television audience. Even though we did not come out with a "W," we came out knowing we were the second-best team in the entire country and would be playing the Asia-Pacific champions, Chinese Taipei, the next day in the third-place consolation game. We Believe.

Our spirits remained high despite our tough loss to Hawaii that night. Knowing we had one more night in the dorms together and a third-place consolation game against Chinese Taipei awaiting us on Sunday morning, we had much to look forward to. However, we also realized our summer to remember was quickly coming to an end. Saturday night began the packing up of our bags, knowing that the next day we'd be with our families embarking on a trip back home to middle Tennessee.

Sunday, August 28th

After our last good night's sleep in the dorms of International Grove, we headed for our last breakfast in the cafeteria before walking over to the indoor cages. We knew today would be an emotional day for all, especially since we had to say our goodbyes to our favorite uncles, Marlin and Chuck. In the cages after our batting practice, Jack presented Uncle Marlin and Uncle Chuck with their own official yellow belts signed by the players and coaches of Tennessee. This sign of gratitude was the least we could do for two men that played such an important part in our Little League World Series experience. As the boys and coaches hugged the uncles, emotions flooded the building and the words, "That's drip," erupted out of Uncle Marlin's and Uncle Chuck's mouths. It was very cool and amusing to see our boys' vernacular having rubbed off on both these uncles.

Before the start of the 3rd place consolation game vs. Chinese Taipei, Mark and I walked over with gloves in hand to the right field line where the boys were warming up. Unfortunately, I didn't get a chance to throw the ball around with William at Lamade Stadium or Volunteer Stadium during the 2021 LLWS, so I had to make sure I took advantage of the opportunity this year. We each played long toss with our sons on the green, immaculate outfield grass of this legendary stadium. Having a catch with William, Jack, and Ella had always been special moments for me over the years, but to throw the ball around with William at the LLWS was truly a moment I'll never forget.

Also, before the national anthem and start of the game, the Chinese Taipei team came over to greet our coaches and players. Despite the language barrier, we shared some laughs, swapped hats, and one of the Chinese Taipei coaches, Phillip Chang, took some candid selfie pictures of both teams hamming it up, which he shared with me. Getting the opportunity to play for third place was a thrill, especially playing an International iconic program like Chinese Taipei.

Team picture with our friends from Chinese Taipei

At last, it was game time and the 37th game of the LLWS was about to start. Because the championship game was taking place at 3:00 p.m. later that day, it was an early 10:00 a.m. start to our game. We were the home team, and our veteran, Jack Rhodes, toed the rubber for Tennessee in our final game of the 2022 Little League World Series. It was a great top of the first inning for Tennessee as Jack induced a fly out and punched out two batters. We couldn't get anything generated in the bottom of the first inning as Chinese Taipei's ace struck out our first three batters: Satinoff, Rhodes, and Daniel.

The top of the second inning started off with a base knock to right field followed by a base on balls. With runners on first and second and none out, Jack got into his zone and blew gas by the next hitter, recording his third strikeout of the game. The next batter hit a comebacker to Jack who alertly turned to third and threw a strike to Chadwick for the second out of the inning. With runners on first and second, the next batter squared to bunt, pulled back, and a double steal was on. Because Drew was charging for the bunt, nobody was covering third, so

Bo quickly threw down to second, but, unfortunately, the ball sailed over Lane's head causing the lead runner to score the first run of the game. Now, with a runner on third with two outs, Jack was able to get out of the jam and strike out the next batter looking. The bottom of the second started off like the previous inning as the first two batters, Wright and Drew, were strikeout victims. Five up and five down as the Chinese Taipei pitcher was dominating our bats with a nasty fast-ball-slider combination. With two outs, Caz stepped to the plate and laid down a beautiful bunt for our first hit of the game. After Logue advanced on a wild pitch to second base, Lane followed with another strikeout on a nasty off-speed pitch.

It was the top of the third and Tennessee was down one. The third inning began with a scorcher hit to Chadwick at third who made a really great play for the first out of the inning. Two consecutive pop ups followed, and Jack was dialed in, throwing another scoreless inning. JF Forni led off the bottom of the third with a strike out, followed by a ground ball out to first by Grayson May. With two outs, Sati stepped up and hit a ground ball down the third base line for a slide in double. As William stood up from his slide, the second baseman came over and congratulated William with a fist bump. This wonderful act of sports-manship was another favorite moment of mine throughout the summer – seeing two Little Leaguers from opposite ends of the world fist bump each other was something special to witness. With William on second and two outs, Jack took a big hack, but went down swinging on a 73 MPH heater. Indeed, a pitching duel for the ages was taking place that morning as, one by one, batters on both sides were being set down.

In the top of the fourth, Chinese Taipei's lead-off batter fisted a floating line drive to centerfield for a base hit. A ground ball to William followed for a 6-4 force out as the batter beat Nash's throw to first denying a double play. Jack's remarkable pitching performance continued as he struck out the next batter swinging for his fifth strikeout of the game. After the runner on first moved up to second on a passed ball, the Chinese Taipei batter hit a blooper in between Sati and Grayson scoring their second run of the game. Jack was able to get out of the inning by inducing a ground ball to Trent at first for the final out of the inning. Bo-Bo led off the bottom of the fourth inning with a long fly ball to right centerfield for a standup double. After getting shut down for most of the game, we had a little pepper going to start the bottom of the fourth. Up next was T-Rex who hit a bouncer back to the mound for a ground out. Unfortunately, the bats couldn't get going as Chinese Taipei's ace kept dealing, striking out Josiah and Caz to end the fourth inning.

Jack walked back to the mound in the top of the fifth inning. The first batter he faced got on with a walk. The following batter hit a ground ball to Nash who flipped it to William for the force out, but the speed of Chinese Taipei's batter beat the throw from William to first negating a 6-4-3 twin killing. That was it for Jack Rhodes. He was at eighty-five pitches, and he had pitched his heart out. We brought in Nash Carter, and he and Jack switched positions. The first batter that Nash faced hit a roller to Jack at second, but trying to turn the double play too quickly, it hit off his glove and runners were safe all around. Like we taught our players since day one, when an error is made, accept it, let your pitcher know it's your bad, and want the next ball. Jack did just that and acknowledged his error and let Nash know. Fortunately, nothing was hurt since the next batter hit a floating line drive to William who threw to Jack at second to double the runner up for the third out. In the bottom of the fifth, we continued to see one of the most dominant pitchers of the summer. Lane and Nash went down swinging for the Chinese Taipei pitcher's eleventh and twelfth strikeouts of the game. Grayson came up with two outs and hit a slow roller back to the mound for the third out of the inning.

Nash came back out for the top of the sixth inning and walked the first batter. The next batter squared to bunt, and Bo popped up behind the dish and made the catch for the first out. The next batter popped up weakly to Nash who fielded his position nicely. With two out, Nash produced a hard-hit ground ball at the hot corner where Drew made a sensational play fielding the short hop and throwing a strike to Jack at second for the third out of the inning. It was now bottom of the sixth inning, and we needed a little bingo, desperately, to keep the inning alive. William started off the bottom of the sixth with a ground ball out to third base. Then, Jack fell victim to another strikeout, Chinese Taipei pitcher's 13th of the game. It was down to Bo Daniel to start the two out rally and keep our hopes alive. Bo ended up hitting a ground ball to second base for the third and final out of the game.

After the customary handshake following the game, we jogged down to the right field line for one last time. With the boys on one knee, Randy delivered his final post-game speech of the year. After Randy concluded, he, unexpectedly, looked at me and asked if I had anything to say. Without a script in hand or any preparation, I told the boys how proud we were of each and every one of them. I also reminded them of the most memorable journey they went on this summer. It wasn't just a journey for this team; it was a journey for their families, our town, and the entire nation to follow. Fortunately, for this group of 13 young men, their families, and us coaches, it will be a journey that will be remembered forever.

Following the game, the team headed back to the dorms to change and finish packing. Despite not winning the last two games, we finished fourth in the world and second in the United States. Winning the Little League World Series was our ultimate goal from the start, but what would come next for this Nolensville Little League team was an honor that is truly second to none. The night before, after our Hawaii loss, the coaches were told that we were the recipients of the 2022 Jack Losch Little League Baseball World Series Team Sportsmanship Award based on our display of sportsmanship on and off the field.

Jack Losch was the centerfielder on the first Little League Baseball World Series Championship team in 1947. He later became a star running back at the University of Miami where he made the record books and was an All-American his senior year in 1955. He starred in three sports (football, baseball, and track) at the University of Miami. One year later, Jack Losch became the first Little League Baseball World Series participant to play a professional sport; The Green Bay Packers selected Losch in the first round of the National Football League amateur draft in 1956.

This award, which started in 2004, is voted on by the 20 participating teams as well as the team hosts, volunteers, media members, and the Little League staff. The Jack Losch Little League Baseball World Series Team Sportsmanship Award recognizes the team that demonstrates an incredible amount of sportsmanship both on and off the field. This includes the team's time in the dormitories, dining hall, and interview room as well as their performance on the diamond. In the past 17 years, only four other United States teams had the privilege of winning this award. Our players and coaches did what we are accustomed to doing: showing respect to others and the game, demonstrating superb sportsmanship on and off the field, and just being considerate human beings. For those qualities and more, I honestly credit the parents who've raised such fine young men.

Several factors were considered by the individuals who voted for the winner of this award, but the one that stood out most was the respect shown by our team throughout the tournament not only to the other teams, but also to the dining room staff, ushers, security personnel, stadium staff, and the great game of baseball itself. Others noticed our compassion towards Snow Canyon Little League's injured player and his Utah team and fans. Others observed our consideration for stadium staff by taking off our muddy cleats before entering the carpeted media interview room during rain delays, and others remembered our expression of love for the game and caring for all others who love it, too, by our interacting with and cheering on the Mason Ohio Youth Organization and Cambrian Park Little League from San Jose California in the 2022 Little League Challenger Division exhibition game. For Randy, Mark, and me, these acts of kindness and displays of great sportsmanship shown by our team were not surprising, but to have these boys especially honored for their behavior was the icing on the cake.

Before the championship game between Hawaii and Curacao, our team made its way to the field to receive the Jack Losch Little League Baseball World Series Team Sportsmanship Award. Dressed in our Little League jerseys, hats, and shorts, we were introduced to the packed crowd. As we walked over to the mound and held the Jack Losch Sportsmanship banner with pride, family members of Jack Losch circled the mound near us.

Presenting the award, the Little League President and CEO said, "The foundation of the Little League program is built around respect, sportsmanship, and the life lessons learned through the game of baseball and softball, and the members of the Nolensville Little League program have exemplified those values throughout the entirety of the World Series this summer. It is my pleasure to present the 2022 Jack Losch Little League Team Sportsmanship Award to Nolensville Little League and thank the players and coaches for exemplifying the spirit of Jack Losch during this year's event." One of the proudest moments for Mark, Randy, and me, during the entire Little League World Series journey, was that moment when we were given that most prestigious award and honor. I can only imagine the pride and joy that our players' parents and families and our fans back home experienced when this acknowledgment was presented.

After receiving this award, some families decided to sign their kids out and start their trek back to Tennessee. We escorted those leaving to the back gate off Fairmont Avenue as they did their final sign outs. However, my family and I stayed to watch the International Championship game, Hawaii defeating Curacao 13-3.

When the championship game concluded, I remember taking my final walk up the steps from Lamade Stadium to the entrance of the International Grove. It was a quiet walk, steps I wanted to remember well since, most likely, it would be the last time I'd ever step foot on the hallowed ground of this most amazing place. I made one final stop to our dorm, checked to make sure everything was picked up, and loaded the golf cart with my luggage. Meg, William, and Jack were waiting in the car outside the back gate. After packing up our vehicle, I brought back the golf cart and dropped off the key at the game room office.

While slowly walking for the final time on the Little League International campus, I smiled with pure delight. Making it to the Little League World Series is once in a lifetime. For William and me to experience it, back-to-back, as father and son is life changing. The on-the-field outcome of the LLWS is really irrelevant. It's the outcome of what lessons were learned, friendships made, and memories of a lifetime created for this special team from Nolensville, their families, and our entire community that will be cherished forever. We Believe.

The drive home from Williamsport with Meg and the boys included lots of reminiscing and reflecting on the past few weeks at the Little League World Series. We also were fortunate enough to stop in Louisville and spend some quality time with Ella on the campus of the University of Louisville.

Once we got home, I anticipated a ton of attention for this Nolensville Little League team, and, boy, did we get just that. A broad array of media appearances followed, along with being distinguished guests at Titans, Vanderbilt Football, Nashville Sounds, Predators, and NASCAR events. Our team was also honored at local city hall meetings, given the key to the town of Nolensville by town officials, and, last but not least, had the opportunity to tour the State Capitol and be congratulated by state senator, Jack Johnson, and Tennessee's governor, Bill Lee. However, all these prestigious events were outdone by the unbelievable community support and parade that followed soon after we got home from Williamsport.

On Wednesday, August 31st, around 6:00 p.m., this amazing town of Nolensville hosted a homecoming parade for our team. All the boys and coaches rode in golf carts and all-terrain vehicles that began in front of the historic school and traveled along a paved path to the Little League complex. Fans of all ages came out and showed their appreciation and support for these hometown heroes. The team, full of smiles, waved to the onlookers and, eventually, ended up under the canopy next to the fields where they signed autographs, took pictures with fans, and soaked up every minute of this special recognition.

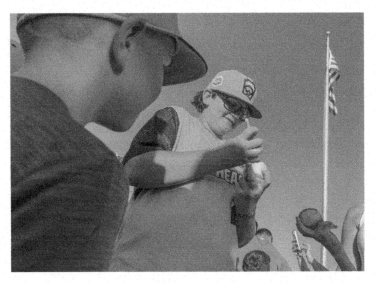

Trent "T-Rex" McNiel signing an autograph for a young fan at the Nolensville LLWS homecoming parade

The summer of 2022 will go down in the history books. If people had told me in the beginning of the Nolensville Little League rec season that this team would be back to the Little League World Series, I probably would have second guessed them. As I reflect on our journey to the Little League World Series, I think of all the life lessons, friendships, and cherished memories throughout the summer. In a world that is filled with too much hatred, divisiveness, and sheer lack of respect for others, a simple game – our national pastime – played by kids brought together teams, fans, and communities from afar. Whether it was players and coaches from around the globe embracing each other's cultures, passionate fans rooting for their favorite teams, or communities uniting to show support for their hometown heroes, the summer of 2022 brought solidarity to all. For the players, coaches, parents, countless fans, and incredible Nolensville community who made this magical summer come true, I thank each and every one of you for allowing me to be just a small part of a journey that will forever be remembered as "We Believe."

THE NOLENSVILLE BOYS OF SUMMER

William Satinoff

Nickname: Sati
Numbers: #1/#9
Positions: SS/P
Bats: R | **Throws:** R
5'3" | 94 lbs.
Favorite MLB Team: Tampa Bay Rays
Favorite MLB Player: Wander Franco

My favorite on-the-field moment was when Jack Rhodes hit the ball down the first base line vs. Goodlettsville in the districts final that scored me with the winning run. Some other favorite moments were in the bottom of the 6th inning, Nash and I turned a game ending double play that sent us to state. In the state tournament after we lost to Columbia, we changed up our saying to "We Believe", and then went on a winning streak beating Columbia in back-to-back games to capture the state championship. Another favorite moment was when the last out was made in the Southeast Regional finals vs. Virginia when Drew tossed me the ball at second, and I stomped on the bag for the double play and final out of the game. The dog pile followed, and we were heading to Williamsport. Lastly, in the LLWS one of my favorite moments was when I made the game saving catch vs. Indiana, and when Josiah hit the grand slam in the first inning vs. Texas, and we ended up winning that game that sent us to the U.S. championship game.

My favorite off-the-field moment was during practices leading up to districts. We would hang out with the team and our families at team dinners at Cabo's and Wings to Go. In the state tournament some of my favorite moments were staying at the cabin with the team, hanging out with the fellas, relaxing in the hot tub, and eating Coach Randy's famous filets. It was also a lot of fun touring the Vanderbilt baseball facility. In regionals, I had a lot of fun hanging out with the team at our hotel and eating team dinners in the hotel conference room. At the LLWS in Williamsport, it was fun meeting and hanging out with the other teams in the International Grove. My two favorite teams to hang out with were Puerto Rico and Texas. I also had a lot of fun chilling with my teammates at our dorm. Hanging out and talking to the teams playing in the Challenger was a really cool experience. I enjoyed watching other teams play at Lamade Stadium and will also always remember hanging out, laughing, and telling Boston Red Sox superstar, Rafael Devers, that the Rays were better than the Red Sox.

My life lesson learned during the LLWS run was how to be a leader, and no matter what your role is, big or small, that each and every player was a special part of this team. I also learned how to better communicate with coaches, teammates, and fans of all ages. It was also a learning moment every time we stood for the national anthem as we respected the flag whether it was on the field or off the field. Lastly, no matter your ability, baseball is a game everyone can love to play.

Grayson May

Nickname: Mullet Man

Numbers: #2/#1

Positions: CF/P

Bats: L | **Throws:** L

4'11" | 75 lbs.

Favorite MLB Team: Atlanta Braves

Favorite MLB Player: Julio Rodriguez

My favorite on-the-field moment was my diving catch during the Massachusetts game! It was cool to see it being shown on ESPN and Barstool Sports.

My favorite off-the-field moment was hanging out with the boys from the other teams. I still keep in touch with some of them!

My life lesson learned during the LLWS run was how cool it was having all the support from the community and fans. My teammates did a good job supporting each other no matter what. I loved being part of a team that really worked well together.

Drew Chadwick

Nicknames: Drewbie, Mountain Drew

Numbers: #10/13

Positions: 3B/P

Bats: R | **Throws:** R

5'4" | 106 lbs.

Favorite MLB Team: Atlanta Braves

Favorite MLB Player: Tim Anderson

My favorite on-the-field moment was during the Virginia game when we went into that game expecting Jack Rhodes to pitch the majority of the game. Unfortunately, after a couple of pitches he started to feel pain in his arm and had to come out. Coach Randy called me over and said you're going to have to go the long way but that he believed in me. I came in trailing throughout the game, but then Virginia's star pitcher had hit the maximum pitch limit. They put in a new pitcher, and we started a rally to take the lead 5-2 going into the 6th. Going into the last inning we had to shut them down. I knew I was reaching my pitch limit but wanted to finish the game. They got a leadoff double, but then we got an out followed by a ground ball. I now had only 10 pitches left to finish the game. There was one out and a runner on second. After nine pitches and a great battle with the hitter, I pitched a fastball on the outside corner and the batter hit a super hard-line drive into the gap. Caz had it played perfectly, caught it, and the runner didn't tag up so he threw it in to Sati to get the runner at 2nd but the ball sailed over his head. Thankfully, I was there to back him up, and it came right to me. I caught it, tossed it to Sati who stomped on second base. We were the Southeast Regional Champions! We all were so happy, and dog piled when we won. I remember Coach Satinoff was so happy, he jumped up and hit his head on the light in the dugout making a dent in it. We took a bunch of pictures, and Coach Randy gave me the game ball. We celebrated at a restaurant with the whole team and the entire restaurant cheered for us.

My favorite off-the-field moment was when we were in the cabin for the state tournament. We had so much fun together. Another favorite moment was the first day we arrived in Williamsport. We got off the bus and I've never been so excited. We got our first look at Lamade stadium from the hilltop, and it was the nicest field I'd ever seen. I couldn't believe we were going to get to play on it. After seeing the field, we met the Mexican team in front of our dorm. It was so cool trying to communicate and learn from them. The excitement from that first night is something I will never forget.

My life lesson learned during the LLWS run was that any team can beat you and you have to be ready no matter if it's Hawaii or if it's McCabe Little League. We learned that the hard way in the state tournament vs Columbia. Losing the first game vs. Columbia really helped our team come together. Another lesson I learned is there is always somebody watching you and that body language is so important. I didn't have a great day at the plate vs. Virginia, but I knew the team needed me on the mound, so I had to stay composed. That helped me so much later in the big games we played in South Williamsport and something I want to keep focusing on.

Wright Martin

Nickname: Wrighty

Numbers: #11/#19

Positions: 1B/P

Bats: R | **Throws:** R

5'11" | 183 lbs.

Favorite MLB Team: Oakland Athletics

Favorite MLB Player: J. J. Schwarz

My favorite on-the-field moment was us beating the Southwest team and knowing we would now have a chance to be in the International Championship.

My favorite off-the-field moment was staying in the dorms with all my friends and just having fun getting to see the international teams.

My life lesson learned during the LLWS run was never underestimate someone and their ability, always be locked in, and put in the most work from anyone around you while outworking everyone... Lastly, never quit.

Jack Rhodes

Nickname: Jack & Cheese
Numbers: #12/#14
Positions: C/P
Bats: R | **Throws:** R
5'8" | 116 lbs.
Favorite MLB Team: Cleveland Guardians
Favorite MLB Player: Jose Ramirez

My favorite on-the-field moment was when I came into pitch versus Good-lettsville in the first game we played them in districts. I remember the crowd just felt electric and behind us. It was so cool to see the 2021 LLWS team all there supporting us and cheering us on! The second time we played Goodlettsville, the crowd's energy was just as high. It was amazing to be on the field and see fireworks light off for us! It was incredible how our friends, family, and the whole community supported us, and we hadn't even won our first tournament! In the championship game at state when I realized my shoulder was hurt, I knew I had to push through it no matter what for my team. Randy calmed me down, helped me get my confidence and put Bio-Freeze on my shoulder to help with the pain. The opening ceremony at the Southeast Regional was so cool, especially when the fighter pilots flew over us. It hyped us up and showed us that this was the real deal! I think the pilots actually created a sonic boom that not only scared us, but our parents saw on the news that a number of homes were damaged because of it. At the LLWS some of my favorite memories included walking on the field to play our first game and seeing the crowd. The much bigger crowd than last year brought so much excitement to me. One of my favorite plays was after the long rain delay against Indiana, we got in a pinch and Sati made an unbelievable diving catch to save the game! Another unforgettable memory was driving to the hospital after getting hit in the wrist by a Hawaii bat. I was so nervous that I wouldn't be there with our team to play Texas. The driver was so nice to me and my mom, and actually gave me a pin from the year that the LLWS didn't happen because of COVID. I was happy when they called and told me I would be fine! Some of my favorite personal moments was hitting twice off Hawaii's ace during the U.S. Championship game and starting against Chinese Taipei was so cool. Pitching against a team from the other side of the world who didn't even speak our language was a real special moment.

My favorite off-the-field moment was when I thought that we were going to make it to the regional again but wasn't confident that we would make it to the Little League World Series once again because I know how lucky we were to have made it the first time. Sati and I weretalking online while playing a video game and were discussing this year's team and if we could make it to the World Series. Sati thought that we could make it, but I told him I didn't think there was any way we could. I was happy to be proven wrong! When we beat South Carolina in the regional, I felt that we could go all the way and do it again. At the state tournament during our stay at the cabin in Goodlettsville, Coach Randy made us an awesome dinner. The bacon wrapped filets were so good! It meant a great deal to us that he cared so much and would make us this special dinner! Another favorite off the field moment was when we went driving after the state championship game in Coach Randy's jeep with some of our team and the Nolensville flag flying out the top! Driving down to Warner Robins, GA, for the Southeast Regional in the Vandy bus was so amazing. We saw South Carolina watch us pull up and their jaws dropped! Randy's slogan in the hotel, "No swimming, no women," made us laugh as we followed this rule! Taking our first day of school pictures in left field during the regional was cool to realize that we were missing school for baseball! While watching another game, I met a boy, his dad, and his friend from Georgia. The dad took his son to regionals every year (except last year because of COVID). The one boy played baseball, but his friend who came for the first time on this trip had just started baseball. I talked with them and asked them a lot of questions. Since one of the boys was just starting baseball, I asked them if they wanted to play catch. We started a friendship that day and for the rest of the entire journey, they cheered us on. They made signs and were at every game! When we made it to the LLWS, their dad sent my parents pictures of them having watch parties and eating mac & cheese to support us! At the LLWS some of my favorite off the field moments included first arriving to Williamsport and meeting Team Mexico in front of our dorms and trying to translate Spanish. Another top moment was for the second time walking to see the fields. Riding on the float and seeing all the people come out to watch and cheer us on was so memorable. From wiffle ball games to playing ping pong with Chinese Taipei for hours the day before we played them, I'll always remember the fun times I had with my team and all the other teams. I'll always remember the Challenger game and how awesome it was to help those kids play the game they love just as much as we do. Before the start of the Challenger game, I got to catch the first pitch from Hall of Famer Rickey Henderson. When I walked the ball to him, I told him he couldn't swipe a bag on me. It was so fun to meet all the MLB players and getting to talk with Trevor Story from the Boston Red Sox. Lastly, leaving Williamsport I was sad knowing our journey was over and that we would never have that experience again. It was the best summer ever!

My life lesson learned during the LLWS run was at the start of the season, people thought that we weren't as strong as last year's team, and it would be very unlikely that we would make it back to Williamsport. This made me turn deep inside myself to believe and work towards achieving this. This summer taught me to believe in myself and my team. I learned to not listen to the doubters but use it as fuel to work even harder to prove them wrong. I also learned that when achievingbig goals-like we did this summer, in every team everyone has an important part whether it is big or small and the roles that we played changed throughout the road. It was important to always step back and look at what our team needed and try to fill that role. Sometimes it was as simple as cheering on another team member who hit a bomb, or picking up a player who made an error, or even swinging the bat the hardest I could toput a ball into play for our team to still have a shot to win.

Josiah Porter

Nickname: Jo-Jo, Big Hand Joe, The Natural

Numbers: #14/#7

Positions: OF/P

Bats: R | **Throws:** R

5'3" | 112 lbs.

Favorite MLB Team: Atlanta Braves

Favorite MLB Player: Freddie Freeman

My favorite on-the-field moment was when I had a few memorable moments on the field, from hitting an important 2-run triple in the state tournament game versus Columbia, to pitching an immaculate inning (9-pitches, 9-strikes, 3-strike-outs) and a perfect 3-innings (9 batters - 9 strikeouts) against Alabama in the Southeast Regional in Warner Robins, to starting the rally in the top of the 5th inning of the Southeast Regional Championship with a bases-empty double off of Virginia's pitcher who had been pretty untouchable the entire game. I went on to score the first run of that game for Nolensville after Wright Martin knocked me in with a single to pull us within 1 run and to help get the pitch count up to the limit. We went on to win the game in the 6th inning (5-2), scoring 4 runs against their reliever, sending us to the Little League World Series in Williams-port. My favorite on the field moment has to be hitting a 1st inning, 2-out, grand slam in the "loser-go-home, winner-goes-to-the-championship" national semifinal game against Pearland, Texas. On ESPN during a prime-time Thursday night game, behind 1-0 in the bottom of the 1st inning, I drilled a 2-1 fastball over the centerfield fence barely missing the Howard J. Lamade statue. We never looked back after that hit and went on to win the game 7-1. Not sure if I had ever had a better moment playing a sport in my life.

My favorite off-the-field moment would probably be all of the time staying with my teammates in the cabin at the state tourney, the hotel at the Southeast Regional in Warner Robins, and the International Grove dorms in Williamsport. Playing video games, pool, arcade games, eating Coach Randy's home-cooked meals, having Lysol and Axe spraying battles, swimming together, playing wiffle ball, and borrowing snacks from each other's rooms. Spending time and bonding with all of my new teammates, who are now my close friends, and meeting new friends from all over the world was just incredibly special. It was also pretty cool doing interviews on national TV and signing autographs. These memories will last a lifetime.

My life lesson learned during the LLWS run was to never give up no matter the circumstances. Respect others, our flag, our country, our freedom, and the people who fought and sacrificed for our freedom. To not focus on the storm (or the bad stuff in life or the things you think you can't do), but instead, focus on the good and never quit trying to do your best and to accomplish great things. It's different for different people, but for me, my faith is very important to me, and so I focus a lot on Jesus. And Jesus gives me strength, hope, and encouragement.

Charlie Malom

Nickname: Chuck Diesel

Numbers: #16/#8

Positions: OF

Bats: R | **Throws:** R

5'6" | 118 lbs.

Favorite MLB Team: St. Louis Cardinals

Favorite MLB Player: Yadier Molina

My favorite on-the-field moment was when we dog piled after beating Columbia in the state tournament.

My favorite off-the-field moment was staying at the dorms playing games and meeting other teams from around the world.

My life lesson learned during the LLWS run was to always have respect and discipline around other people.

Nash Carter

Nickname: Nasher

Numbers: #18/#3

Positions: MI/P

Bats: L | **Throws:** R

4'10" | 85 lbs.

Favorite MLB Team: Atlanta Braves

Favorite MLB Player: Dansby Swanson

My favorite on-the-field moment was when Josiah hit the grand slam against Texas. I was on deck and standing on the stairs in the first base dugout. When he hit it, everyone stormed out of the dugout to celebrate with him. My favorite LLWS personal moment was when Sati and I turned the double play against Texas. It was a hard ground ball to Sati; he made a good play, and we turned it before the batter got to first. It wasn't my favorite moment in regionals, but my most memorable moment was pitching for the first time on TV against Georgia. I threw up before and during the game because I was so nervous. I came in to pitch during the second inning and allowed one run but somehow held them the rest of the game.Looking back on it, it was funny tripping Wright right before the dog pile. You have to watch it back to really see what I am talking about. It started the pile! During the state, we got beat by Columbia early in the tourney and then smoked them the last few games. Getting to dog pile after we won and celebrate after the game with each other, and our families, and friends was a lot of fun. I like looking back at those photos. I hit and pitched pretty good at state. Pitching that last state championship game was probably the most memorable personally. Our last game I had to come in for Trent early in the game and was able to shut Columbia down the rest of the game. During districts, when Drew hit the walk-off double to beat Goodlettsville the first time we played them was a cool team memory. My favorite personal moment from the district tournament was when Sati and I turned the double play to win the championship against Goodlettsville.

My favorite off-the-field moment was hanging out with the other teams at the LLWS. It was fun to try and communicate with Curacao. I also really enjoyed getting to play and hang out with Texas and Massachusetts in the game room and wiffle ball field. During regionals, we ended up becoming buddies with South Carolina. I enjoyed hanging out with them in the hotel. We had a tough game against them, but it was fun to see them cheer us on even after we put them out. They were a team filled with good guys. I really liked them. Other than going to the LLWS, our time together at state and getting to stay with each other at the cabin was the most fun we had as a team other than playing the games. I think of the fun times we had in our rooms, and also, the bacon wrapped filets Coach Randy cooked. They were very good...the best I have ever had! During districts we often went to Cabos after practices and wins. It was fun because it was a fun place we got to hang out with each other and our parents.

My life lesson learned during the LLWS run was embracing every moment with teammates and coaches. That was a great lesson we all learned because we will probably never have the opportunity to play with the same group of guys ever again. During regionals, I was super nervous in the Georgia game and actually threw up twice (once before the game and once during it). The next time I find myself being nervous about something I will think back to that game and remind myself that everything is going to be okay. In the state tournament we lost to Columbia early in the tournament, but we never gave up. We took the rest of the tournament one pitch at a time, one day and game at a time, and eventually played that same team again and beat them twice, badly. So, the lesson is to never give up. In district play, I challenged myself by playing in the Nolensville little league and trying to make the all-star team knowing there was a chance I may not make it. So, putting yourself in a position to possibly fail is something you should push yourself to do because if you do succeed it will be very worth it and maybe even life changing.

JF Forni

Nickname: JF

Numbers: #20/#2

Positions: OF

Bats: R | **Throws:** R

5'0" | 80 lbs.

Favorite MLB Team: Atlanta Braves

Favorite MLB Player: Ronald Acuna Jr.

My favorite on-the-field moment was my at bat in the Goodlettsville game during districts. I got on base with a single and was the tying run. We rallied and scored some runs to win the game! Drew then closed the game, and we were headed to state!!!

My favorite off-the-field moment was hanging out at the cabin we stayed in overnight during state. We really got to know each other so well during those couple days. That was so awesome. Another favorite off the field moment was hanging out with the team from Texas during the LLWS.

My life lesson learned during the LLWS run was hanging out with all the fellas for so many days made me a better man. I learned during the several months of little league that you should never give up on a dream.

Lane Dever

Nickname: Lane-O
Numbers: #22/#4
Positions: OF/2B
Bats: R | **Throws:** R
5'1" | 99 lbs.
Favorite MLB Team: Washington Nationals
Favorite MLB Player: Bryce Harper

My favorite on-the-field moment was how we came back in the final game of regionals, dog piled after the win, and our lap around the field. Another favorite moment was the celebration after we beat Goodlettsville when the fireworks went off. Another favorite was the dog pile after state and how we just couldn't believe that we were going to Warner Robins to play baseball at the field we had watched on TV for years. The first game on the field was so perfect, and the in-ground dugout was amazing. One more favorite moment was when we beat Texas to go to the U.S. championship and the grand slam that Jo-Jo hit to put us out in front early. My favorite personal moment was when I hit the double against Texas, and coach Randy called it!

My favorite off-the-field moment was definitely seeing Lamade Stadium for the first time and the bus rides to Warner Robins and Williamsport. Another favorite off the field moment was going to all the games when we could and talking to the international teams from all over the world. The cabin in Goodlettsville was a ton of fun. After we played our games in regionals and the LLWS we would all watch ourselves on TV. The walk around the field and the stadium the first day we got there was so much fun. We had the best uncles at LLWS and the walks to the practice facility while walking through hundreds of people and signing autographs were some of my other favorite off-the field moments.

My life lesson learned during the LLWS run was to always follow your dreams and never give up.

Bo Daniel

Nickname: Bo-Bo
Numbers: #27/#5
Positions: C/OF/P
Bats: R | **Throws:** R
5'5" | 103 lbs.
Favorite MLB Team: Houston Astros
Favorite MLB Player: Alex Bregman

My favorite on-the-field moment was when I hit a grand slam at regionals against Georgia in the semi-final game. In the first inning, they got up 2-0; we got three outs after we changed pitchers from Jack to Nash after Jack's arm started hurting. We were up to bat the next inning when Sati got walked. Jack got hit, and Drew followed with a walk, leaving the bases loaded for me up to bat. Georgia's pitcher threw me a pitch right down the middle and I turned my hips and swung the bat at the ball. It flew right over the fence. I remember stopping at second base thinking it was a ground-rule double.

My favorite off-the-field moment was when we would go to eat breakfast, lunch, and dinner in the cafeteria in Williamsport. In the morning, we would get woken up by Coach Evan's animal calls, then have a few minutes to get our credentials and clothes on and head down to the cafe. We would grab our breakfast from the buffet-looking thing and then sit at our table. It was always so fun to eat as a team every day.

My life lesson learned during the LLWS run was to communicate with people and make friends. I had interviews, and for them, I had to understand how to communicate and converse with people. I had to learn to make friends with people I have never seen before in my life. I will be impacted by these life lessons throughout my life.

Caz Logue

Nickname: Cazzy
Numbers: #31/#6
Positions: OF/3B/P
Bats: L | **Throws:** R
5'4" | 114 lbs.
Favorite MLB Team: Atlanta Braves
Favorite MLB Player: Austin Riley

My favorite on-the-field moment was in the regional championship game when I had an RBI single against Virginia to put us ahead in the last inning.

My favorite off-the-field moment was staying in the dorms in Williamsport. I think our team really got a lot closer then. We had so much fun playing wiffle ball and ping pong. I also really liked hanging out and meeting the other teams, especially the international teams.

My life lesson learned during the LLWS run was that my coaches taught us to stay calm and breathe during tough times. We really did that during all of our games and never gave up. This is a life lesson that I can continue doing throughout playing sports and even when I'm an adult working.

Trent McNiel

Nickname: T-Rex

Numbers: #33/#20

Positions: P/1B

Bats: L | **Throws:** R

5'8" | 201 lbs.

Favorite MLB Team: St. Louis Cardinals

Favorite MLB Player: Yadier Molina

My favorite on-the-field moment was pitching in the U.S. championship game and striking out two of the best hitters in the tournament.

My favorite off-the-field moment was meeting players from other countries and getting to interact and play ping-pong with them.

My life lesson learned during the LLWS run was how to stand correctly for the National Anthem, and being humble, knowing that most kids never get this opportunity.

2022 Nolensville Little League 12u All-Stars

District 7 Champions

Tennessee State Champions

Southeast Region Champions

2nd in the Nation and 4th in the World

Jack Losch Little League Baseball World Series Team Sportsmanship Award

Southeast standing for the National Anthem during the U.S. Championship

Jack, Ella, and William

Always Believe.

ACKNOWLEDGMENTS

I owe a lot of gratitude and love to many people that helped make this memoir a reality.

To Randy Huth and Chris Mercado...thank you for welcoming me into the Nolensville Little League All-Star family back in the fall of 2020. Without your trust and belief in me, this whole experience wouldn't have been a reality.

To the Nolensville community...what a ride it's been the last two summers; the enthusiasm, support, and team spirit you've demonstrated was unparalleled. I am confident that there will be more LLWS appearances for Nolensville in years to come.

To Avery Sports Photos, Charles Pulliam, Mark Carter, Craig Dever, and our many other parents... thank you for capturing priceless moments of our LLWS journey and allowing me to highlight those moments with your photos in this memoir.

To all the players; coaches, Randy Huth, Chris Mercado, Mark Carter; and families of the 2021 and 2022 teams...the memories and friendships we've held over the last two years will stay cherished forever.

To my mother-in-law, Peggy Jennings...this memoir wouldn't be complete without the love, care, and proofreading from you. Thank you, Mom, for all the countless hours spent editing *We Believe*.

To my mom, dad, and brother. . .if it weren't for the three of you, the game I love so much wouldn't be such a big part of who I am today. . .much love and appreciation.

Lastly, to my wife, Meg; kids, Ella, Jack, and William. . .since the beginning, baseball has been such a vital part of our family. Thank you for allowing me to share the great game of baseball every day with you, and for your continued support while I wrote this memoir. . .love you all.